CONTEMPORARY
machine embroidery

CONTEMPORARY

machine embroidery

DEBORAH GONET

Chilton
BOOK COMPANY

RADNOR, PENNSYLVANIA

CONTEMPORARY MACHINE EMBROIDERY

For Pat and Frank

First published in the United States of America in 1996
by Chilton Book Company, Radnor, Pennsylvania

First published in Great Britain in 1996 by Mitchell Beazley
an imprint of Reed Consumer Books Limited
Michelin House, 81 Fulham Road, London SW3 6RB
and Auckland, Melbourne, Singapore and Toronto
Copyright © 1996 Reed International Books Limited
Text copyright © Reed Consumer Books Limited
Photography copyright © Reed Consumer Books Limited
Craft design and artwork copyright © Deborah Gonet

Art Director *Gaye Allen*
Executive Art Editor *Janis Utton*
Executive Editor *Judith More*
Senior Art Editor *Susan Downing*
Co-ordinating Editor *Anthea Snow*
Designer *Bobbie Colgate Stone*
Editor *Heather Dewhurst*
Photographer *Carol Sharp*
Illustrators *Deborah Gonet, Kuo Kang Chen*
Indexer *Ann Barrett*
Production Controller *Juliette Butler*

ISBN 0-8019-8754-7

Set in Bembo and Futura
Produced by Mandarin Offset
Printed in Hong Kong

CONTENTS

INTRODUCTION

I HAVE BEEN INTERESTED in embroidery from an early age. As a child, I was often given craft kits and encouraged by my family to develop my interest and love in making and decorating things. My mother was a great inspiration to me. As she had a large family, she was always making something, whether sewing clothes, curtains, or chair covers, knitting sweaters, or producing wonderful embroidery. I loved watching her at work and then trying it out for myself. At the age of 13, I started making my own clothes, which my mother cheerfully encouraged. I wanted to have as many fashionable clothes as possible and making my own was a fun and economical way of going about it.

As a natural progression from this early interest, I decided to pursue textile design as a career. At college in Glasgow and then in London, I studied both embroidered and woven textiles. It was in my last year that I realized embroidery was my greatest love. The immediacy with which you can transform a plain piece of fabric into something rich and beautiful is what continues to excite me.

During my time at college I became engrossed and fascinated by the fashion world, spending many hours perusing books and visiting museums to look at their dress and textile collections of the past and present. Art galleries provided inspiration, too – the splendor and grandeur of the garments worn in the 17th and 18th centuries are wonderfully captured in the paintings at London's National Portrait Gallery.

Two designers who influenced me greatly at this time were Elsa Schiaparelli and Christian Lacroix. I loved their sense of design and lavishly embellished garments,

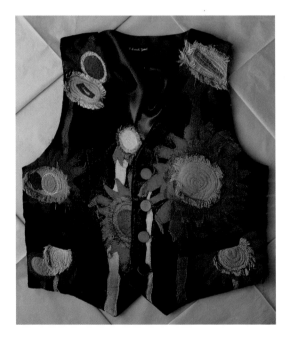

and wanted to capture that opulence and create textiles and garments that were constructed entirely of embroidery. Stitching was to be the important component rather than just a decoration.

On leaving college, I set up my own business making and selling initially vests – and then shirts, scarves, bags, and cushions, as well. I also produced wall hangings, quilts, curtains, and wedding dresses. A vest is a wonderful vehicle for embroidery and allows for many design possibilities. This versatile yet simple garment is suitable for many occasions. It is warm, practical, and yet always in fashion. The surface area of a vest is small and fitted, and therefore, it does not need to flow. This can widen the choice of fabrics and the type and amount of embellishment open to you as a machine embroiderer.

The very first vest I produced was inspired by heraldry, with its traditional symbols, patterns, and bright colors. Old books, paintings, wall hangings, and fabrics can be an exciting source of inspiration – and putting traditional designs together in new ways offers a challenge to any designer.

I planned the arrangement of the design around the shape of the vest, considering the scale and position of the bold imagery. Then, using a sewing machine as my drawing tool, I recreated these heraldic symbols in many textures and colors on a gold silk base which further enhanced the overall design. I really enjoyed making this vest and the finished result was so frequently complimented and admired so frequently that I was motivated to design and sell them. My business began simply by producing what I wanted to wear, and I have continued in a true labour of love.

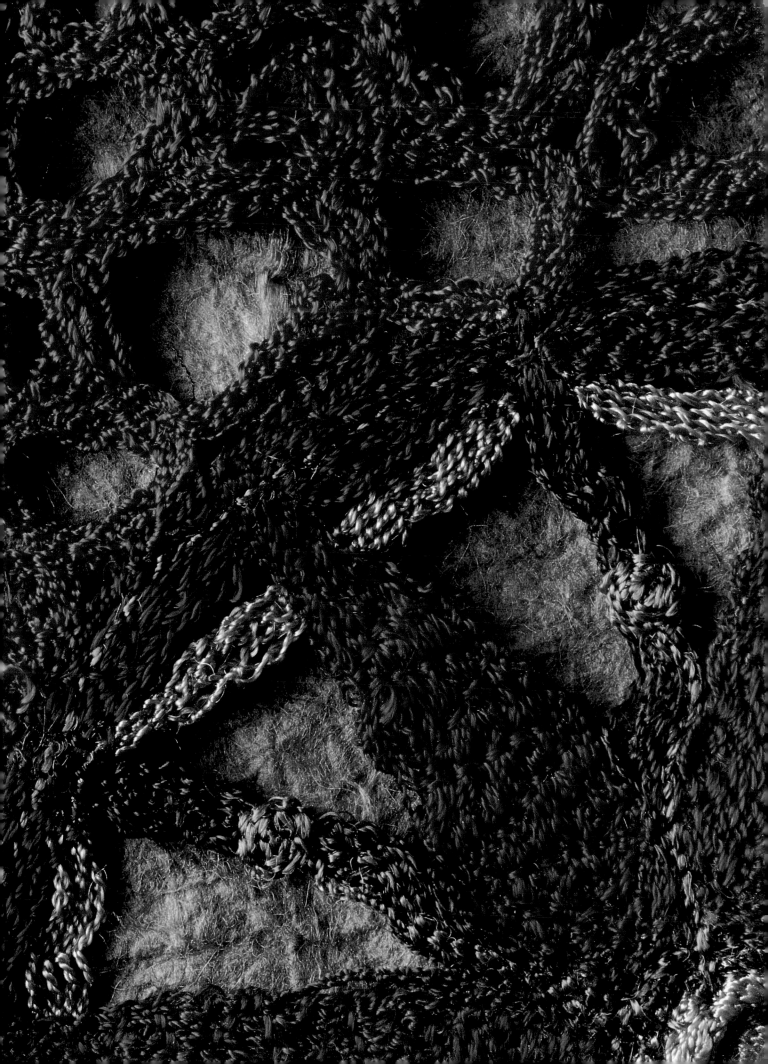

DESIGN INSPIRATION

MY DESIGNS are inspired by a huge variety of sources, the world of nature being one of them. Being brought up in Scotland, I was surrounded by a wealth of colors, patterns, and textures in the magnificent rolling landscape. The hills covered in heather and bracken, and the wonderfully dramatic skies still inspire me today. Nature's color palette is varied and extensive, ranging from bright iridescent tones to soft pale shades. The subtle mixes and unusual color combinations are what I find so appealing and captivating.

Flowers are another natural spur to the imagination, with their wonderful array of enticing colors, the luminosity and transparency of their petals and leaves, their velvety textures and complex structures. I love large, showy flowers in punchy colors, and I have used interpretations of these for many projects. I find spring and summer a wonderfully rich source of inspiration, when we are intoxicated by the heady fragrances of flowers and stimulated by the spectacular array. I refer to this source again and again, either using just the colors or interpretations of the structures. The changing beauty of foliage throughout the year is spectacular, supplying a wonderfully warm color palette that ranges from luscious greens and yellows to rich russets, oranges, and reds. Images that always excite me are the many varieties of majestic trees, such as oaks and elms, and the flowing shapes of willows and vines.

Iridescent tropical fish and strange underwater creatures existing in coral reefs, with their exquisite colors and patterns, have always intrigued me. In particular, I am fascinated by corals and sea anemones, with their flower-like arrangements and amazing structures. Although the animal world is not a source I look to regularly for ideas, I do occasionally see something stirring, such as the vivid coloring, markings, and patterns of snakes, birds, and butterflies.

I have a passion for early illustrations, engravings, and maps, depicting the sun, moon, stars, planets, comets, celestial bodies, and other other wonders of the sky. The warm opulent colors, and the composition and ideas behind these illustrations, are very stimulating. In the same way, I have regularly used the graphic shapes and faded, distressed colors of old-fashioned children's toys and board games as a source of creative ideas.

Aerial photography is a unique medium for colors and patterns, in which ordinary everyday objects, structures, and landscapes are transformed into beautiful multicolored designs. Fields of crops, plowed furrows, and meadows appear like a huge patchwork quilt spread over the land. They are full of fabulous patterns and a subtle, earthy color palette.

Heraldry is a very exciting subject, full of symbolism, and one I refer to a great deal. I like the simple geometric shapes and bold colors used to achieve striking patterns, and the fantastical monsters, animals, birds, and flora which are used as heraldic devices.

Decorative wrought ironwork always inspires me. I find it very beautiful and have designed many pieces using this abundant source of ideas. The Victoria and Albert Museum in London has a wonderful gallery displaying many examples of gates, panels, railings, and household objects. What appeals to me is the ornate quality of the ironwork, with its flowing forms and shapes. Icons and all forms of jewelry provide another rich, creative source. I love the detail in really encrusted, ornate pieces. Jewels, gemstones, and enamels give me an intense, lustrous color palette.

Paintings provide wonderful examples of how to use composition and color. I admire and refer constantly to artists such as Sonia Delaunay, Marc Chagall, Paul Klee, Friedensreich Hundertwasser, Vincent Van Gogh, Claude Monet, Raoul Dufy, Pablo Picasso, and Bridget Riley. All use color in clever, powerful, and imaginative ways. Hundertwasser is a favorite of mine and one who inspires me greatly. I love the lush opulence of his colors, his simple interpretations of nature, his composition of patterns and images, and, above all, the energy and flamboyance of his paintings.

Likewise, folk art, with its basic shapes, forms, and colors, has always brought me great pleasure. The simplicity of the designs and use of pure color are its charms. The exploration of geometric shapes frequently figures in my work. I enjoy manipulating scale, color, and shapes to devise interesting combinations.

Traditional methods of needlework, such as drawn threadwork, lacemaking, patchwork, appliqué, and goldwork, are fascinating to me. I am attracted to objects that have been created with much care and attention to detail, and am constantly amazed at the time and skill that were lovingly bestowed on them.

I enjoy recreating these techniques using a sewing machine, which is faster and gives the pieces a more up-to-date look, while striving to retain the qualities that attracted me to them.

Finally, the fabrics and threads that I use in my work are an inspiration in themselves. There is an abundant supply of marvelously rich fabrics in a huge choice of colors, from subtle pale shades to brilliant vibrant ones, readily available. The fabrics I like to use are silks, which feel fabulous and drape beautifully, linens for their tactile quality, and velvets for their luxuriance and elegance. Rayon embroidery threads have an excellent lustrous quality and come in an enormous color range, while metallic threads add definite sparkle and glamour.

I am always looking for new and unusual source material, keeping my eyes open for inspiring colors, shapes, and textures. I often go to museums and exhibitions, sketching and taking photographs of anything that catches my eye. I collect books, postcards, magazine articles and any other visual source that I find appealing or suitable. This is my reference material which I pin on a boards and lay out in front of me, letting the images soak in.

When I was asked to write this book and share my experience of embroidery, I was flattered and delighted. My love for what I do is what motivates me, and I enjoy sharing that with others. I hope that you will derive as much pleasure making these projects as I have had in creating them, and that they will give you the confidence to invent your own designs.

CLOTHING AND ACCESSORIES

CIRCLES SHIRT

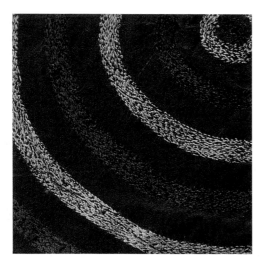

THIS SHIRT TAKES as its inspiration the artist Friedensreich Hundertwasser's interpretation of trees. Circles within circles in bold, bright colors are truly wonderful in their simplicity, combined with delicate spiral motifs that have been inspired by wrought ironwork. The design is similar to the patterns and borders used on tiled floors by the early Greeks and Romans, and has been used here as a border on the hem of the shirt. The resulting design, a row of concentric circles placed side by side in two-color combinations, has a light and airy quality. The lines of stitching allow the background color of the shirt to enhance the design, and the fabric's natural fluidity to be retained.

EQUIPMENT AND MATERIALS

Basic sewing kit (see page 124)

4½yd (4m) burgundy silk crêpe
de Chine

Dark-purple, light-purple, dark-green,
and light-green rayon threads

1⅜yd (1.2m) lightweight iron-on
interfacing

4 x burgundy silk thread

4 x ¾in (19mm) self-cover buttons

◆ *Enlarge the templates by 495%*

1 Enlarge the pattern on page 135 as instructed. Decide on the length of your shirt, and shorten or lengthen your pattern pieces where indicated. Measure the length of fabric required for the 1-Front and 2-Back pattern pieces. Lay out the silk on a flat surface, measure the length required for the 1-Front, add 10in (25cm) and cut. Repeat for the 2-Back piece. Place the patterns on both pieces of fabric with the extra length at the bottom of the shirt. Using tailor's chalk, draw a line where the pattern ends. Then remove the pattern, measure 6.5cm (2½in) up from the

chalk line, and draw a faint line with the chalk; this is where the shirt's embroidered border will start.

2 Enlarge the templates to the correct size. Place a sheet of tissue paper on top and trace the design with a pencil. Do this for both the 1-Front and 2-Back pieces, leaving a space in between the two front sections. Place each template section on the fabric above the faint chalk line, and pin securely in place.

3 Using the burgundy silk thread, stitch around the design with a single line of running stitches. Carefully tear away the paper (see the diagram). Untighten the screw of an embroidery hoop to make it quite loose and place it around the silk. Tighten the hoop, being careful not to make it too tight, as this will mark the fabric.

Before you start embroidering the border for the shirt, practice stitching the design on a spare piece of fabric to get a feel for the amount of stitching required to maintain a nice tension.

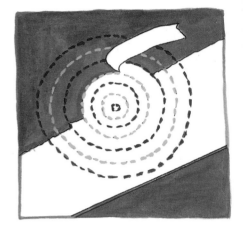

Use rayon or soft thin cotton thread in the bobbin, and be careful not to make the stitching too dense, as this makes the fabric very hard. Once you feel confident with the technique, start embroidering the shirt.

4 Following the design and colour plan, embroider as follows:
Dark purple Starting in the middle of a circle, embroider the central dot using running stitch. Stitch a series of close circles in a spiral pattern until the area is filled. Then go to every alternate ring and fill in the area marked

TEMPLATES / DESIGN AND COLOR PLAN FOR FRONT

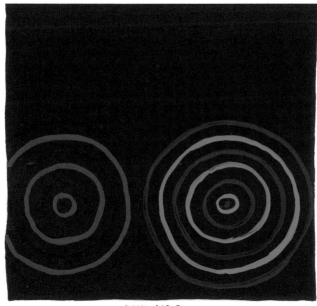

←————16¼in/40.5cm————→   ←————16¼in/40.5cm————→

with 10 to 15 rows of stitching.

Light purple Stitch the rings that are left, as above, until you have completed the seven rings of the circle (see the diagram).

Dark green Move to the next circle, and repeat as for the dark purple above.

Light green Repeat as for the light purple above.

Repeat this embroidery on the shirt until all the circles on both the front and the back pieces have been embroidered. Remove the embroidery hoop carefully and press the fabric with a steam iron.

ASSEMBLY

Cut out the embroidered 1-Front and 2-Back pieces. Cut out the 3-Front facing, 4-Back neck facing, and 5-Sleeve pieces in fabric. Cut out pieces 3 and 4 in interfacing. Fuse the interfacing to the wrong side of the 3-Front facings and the 4-Back neck facings.

Pin the upper edges of the 1-Front and 2-Back pieces together, with right sides facing, and stitch using burgundy silk thread. Make a flat fell seam (see Basic Techniques page 130). Pin the 3-Front and 4-Back neck facings together at the shoulders. Turn in the seam allowance along the unnotched edge and press. Stitch close to the pressed edge, then trim. Pin the facing to the front opening and neck edges, matching seams. Stitch, trim, and clip the seam. Open out the facing and stitch it to the seam allowance, close to the seam. Turn the facing to the inside, and press. Baste at the shoulder seams.

Pin the 5-Sleeve to the armhole edge, with right sides together and notches matching. Stitch, then stitch

again 6mm (¼in) from the seam allowance. Trim close to the stitching. Press the seam toward the sleeve.

Pin the 1-Front and 2-Back pieces together at the sides. Pin the 5-Sleeve edges together. Stitch these in one continuous seam, ending where marked. Turn the side self-facings to the inside along the foldlines, turning in ¼in (6mm) along the outer edges, and press. Turn up a 2in (5cm) sleeve hem and press. Turn in ¼in (6mm) on the edge, press, and stitch. Repeat with the second sleeve.

Open out the front and side facings. Turn up a 2in (5cm) hem, and press. Turn in ¼in (6mm) on the edge, press, and stitch. Turn in the front facings, and slipstitch to the hem. Slipstitch the lower edges together. Turn in the side facings, and pin. Stitch around all the edges and across the top. Slipstitch the lower edges together.

Make four buttonholes on the right front at the markings. Cover the buttons in some of the spare silk (see page 83 for instructions) and sew onto the left front at the markings.

TEMPLATE / DESIGN AND COLOR PLAN FOR BACK

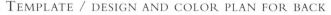

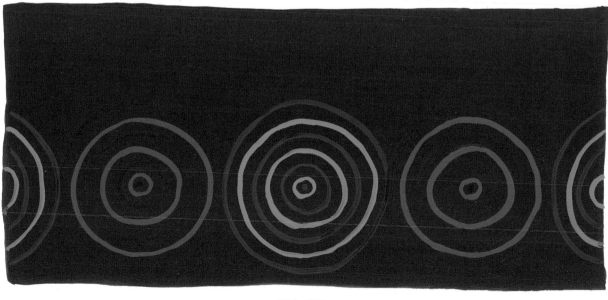

— 31½in/79cm —

FLOWERS SHIRT

THE LACY EMBROIDERY on this shirt is reminiscent of many decorative patterns, including wrought ironwork, traditional drawn threadwork, and circle and flower motifs. The delicate lacy effect is achieved by using dissolvable fabric. This allows you to execute a design that is composed entirely of stitching, once the fabric holding the embroidery has been dissolved. The intense color palette of the panels uses the brilliant golden-yellow and turquoise, and the glowing purple and reds, of jewels and gemstones, which contrast with the dark-indigo silk georgette of the shirt. The overall statement is one of sophistication and refinement.

EQUIPMENT AND MATERIALS
Basic sewing kit (see page 124)
1¼yd (1m) hot-water dissolvable fabric
Yellow, purple, burgundy, dark-green,
    leaf-green, orange, dark-purple,
    turquoise, red, teal, and indigo
    rayon threads
5¼yd (4.5m) indigo silk crêpe georgette
4 x indigo silk threads
5 x ⅝in (15mm) self-cover buttons

◆ *Enlarge the templates by 107%*

1 Enlarge the pattern on page 136, as
instructed. Decide on the length of
your shirt and shorten or lengthen the
pattern pieces where indicated. Measure
the length of the 1–Front; this will be
the length of the panels. Enlarge the
panel template to the correct size and
make six copies. Join three copies
together lengthwise, then repeat with
the other three. Join the pieces together
side by side. Measure your required
length, and finish the bottom edge with
a ½in (1cm) border, as at the top edge.

2 Enlarge and make two copies of
the cuff template. Place all of the
templates on a flat surface next to each
other and fix with masking tape. Place
the hot-water dissolvable fabric on top.
Measure 4in (10cm) down from the
top and in at the sides of the fabric,
and position it so that the templates are
within this space. Anchor the fabric to
the surface with masking tape. (This is
to ensure that pieces do not move while
you trace the design.)

3 Trace the design onto the hot-
water dissolvable fabric with a
pencil. Beginning with the panels,
place the fabric in an embroidery hoop,
making sure that the panels are straight.
Before you start embroidering them,
practice using the dissolvable fabric as
directed in the Basic Techniques
section (see page 128). Once you feel
confident with the technique, start on
the shirt panels, following steps 4–9.
Then repeat for the two cuffs.

TEMPLATE FOR CUFFS

TEMPLATE FOR PANELS

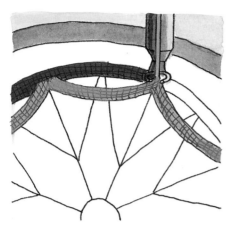

4 Following the design and color plan on pages 20–21, embroider the first circle (on the far left) as follows:

Yellow Stitch the outline of the shape, then fill in with horizontal and vertical rows of stitching, to guarantee that there is dense coverage.

Purple Stitch the outline of the circle, catching in the points of the yellow stitching (see the diagram), then fill in the shape. Move to the star and stitch the outline, then fill in the shape.

Burgundy Stitch the other four points of the star shape as above.

Dark green Stitch eight lines out from the middle of the star; fill in the shape.

Leaf green Starting in the middle of the star and stitch a line on top of the dark green band. Before the edge, embroider a dot, then return to the middle. Repeat the process on each of the green bands. Stitch a circle on top of the purple outer circle, embroidering a dot at the point of every purple star.

← 11¼in/28cm →

2⅜in/6cm

← 13¼in/33cm x 3   Total length 39½in/99cm →

3½in/9cm

Yellow Embroider the central circle. **Dark green** Embroider the figure "2" on top of the yellow circle.

5 Following the plan, embroider the second circle as follows:
Orange Stitch the outline of the central circle, the radiating lines, and the outer circle; then fill in.
Dark purple Stitch the outline of the central circle, the ten radiating lines, and the two outer circles, then fill in.
Turquoise Stitch around the purple inner circle five times, then stitch a small line ¼in (5mm) long on the radiating lines. Stitch the outline of the ten radiating lines (on top of the orange lines) and outer circles (web), and fill in.

6 Following the plan, embroider the third circle as follows:
Burgundy Stitch the outline of the central circle, six radiating lines, and the outer circle, then fill in.

Red Stitch the two circles, using three lines of stitching and embroidering on top of the burgundy lines.
Teal Stitch the outline of the petals, then fill in, leaving the middles open.
Red Stitch four lines of stitching through the middle of each petal.
Yellow Stitch a line from the middle to the outer red circle on each red line, stitch a dot, and return to the middle.

7 Following the plan, embroider the fourth circle as follows:
Red Stitch the outline of the eight-pointed star and outer circle, and fill in.
Yellow Stitch the outline of the central circle, leaving a space between the red and yellow circles. Then stitch eight sun rays, on top of the red, and fill in.
Turquoise Fill in the central circle, then stitch a single line through the middle of the red points. Stitch around the outline of the outer circle and fill in, merging in with the red circle.

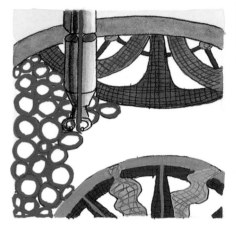

8 Embroider the space between circles 3 and 4, and 4 and 1 with orange circles. Stitch a circle and then go around the shape with five rows of stitching. Stitch another one beside it, joining the sides (see the diagram) and continue until the space is filled.

9 Embroider the borders as follows:
Indigo Fill in the border with horizontal and vertical stitches. Make

DESIGN AND COLOR PLAN FOR CUFFS

DESIGN AND COLOR PLAN FOR PANELS

sure that you cover the area densely, since it needs to be fairly strong.
Burgundy Stitch a zigzag line down the middle of the border with two rows of stitching.

Continue embroidering until you have completed both panels and cuffs. When you have finished, check over the stitching on all the pieces. Make sure that there are no loose stitches and finish off any ends.

10 Dissolve the fabric as directed in Basic Techniques (see page 128). This will cause the embroidered panels to shrink slightly. The piece is ready when soft and pliable. Leave it to dry flat then press with a steam iron.

ASSEMBLY

Cut out the pattern pieces 1, 2, 3, 4, 5, 6, and 7 from the silk georgette.

Stitch two of the fabric pieces for 6 together, and two of the pieces for 7, leaving one piece of each remaining. (This is used instead of interfacing, which would be visible through the georgette, to strengthen the fabric.)

Lay the two 1-Front pieces on a flat surface. Measure 4¼in (10.5cm) from the front openings, place the panels here and pin in place. Stitch using the indigo rayon thread. Go over the edges with satin stitch, set at stitch width 3 and stitch length 0.5.

Pin the sides of the embroidered cuffs together and stitch. Go over the edges with satin stitch, set at stitch width 3 and stitch length 0.5.

Turn up the 2-Back hem by 2in (5cm) and press. Turn in ¼in (6mm) on the edge, press, and stitch using the indigo silk thread (continue with this thread). Pin the upper edges of the 1-Front and 2-Back pieces right sides together, and stitch. Make a flat fell seam, following the instructions in

Basic Techniques (see page 130).

Pin 3-Left Fly to the left front opening, matching notches. Stitch and trim. Press the seam toward the fly. Turn up a 2in (5cm) hem on the left and fly front, and press. Turn in ¼in (6mm) on the edge, press, and stitch. Turn in the long unnotched edge of the left fly along the outer foldline. Sew invisibly along the edge. Turn to the inside along the foldline and press. Slipstitch the pressed edge over the seam and lower edges together. Baste across the upper edge.

Stitch 3-Left Fly close to the seam. Pin 4-Right Fly to the right front

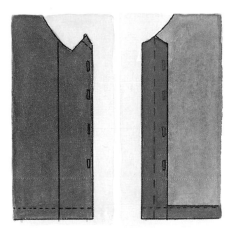

opening, matching notches. Stitch and trim. Press the seam toward the fly.

Turn up a 2in (5cm) hem on the right and fly front, and press. Turn in ¼in (6mm) on the edge, press, and stitch. Turn in the long unnotched edge of the right fly along the outer foldline. Baste across upper and lower edges. Make four buttonholes at the markings.

To form the fly, turn the right fly to the inside along the remaining foldline. Press, then baste along the stitching line. Stitch the 4-Right Fly close to the seam (see the diagram). Turn the facing over the stitching. Press, then baste across the upper edge, and slipstitch the lower edges together. Baste the fly to

1-Front between each buttonhole. Stitch around the neck edge ⅛in (3mm) from the seam allowance.

Stitch the 7-Collar sections together, leaving the notched edge open, and trim. Turn right side out. Press, then baste the raw edges together. Turn in the seam allowance on the single notched edge of the 6-Collar Band. Press, and trim the seam allowance to ⅜in (1cm). Pin the 6-Collar Band to both sides of the 7-Collar. Stitch, leaving the neck edge open. Trim, turn right side out, and press.

Pin the 6-Collar Band to the neck edge, matching notches, and clip where necessary. Stitch, keeping the pressed edge free. Trim and clip the seam. Press the seam toward the 6-Collar Band. Slipstitch the pressed edge over the seam. Edge-stitch the collar band.

Pin 5-Sleeve to the armhole edge, with right sides together and matching the notches. Stitch, making a flat fell seam (see Basic Techniques page 130), and press. With wrong sides together, pin the 1-Front and 2-Back together at the sides, then pin the 5-Sleeve edges together. Stitch in a continuous French seam (see Basic Techniques, page 130), ending where marked, and press. Turn the side self-facings to the inside along the foldlines, turning in ¼in (6mm) along the outer edges, and press.

Pin the cuff to the sleeve hem, making little pleats around the edge until it fits. Stitch, then trim the seam close to the edge. Using the indigo rayon thread, go over the edges with satin stitch, set at stitch width 3 and stitch length 0.5.

Make a buttonhole on the right collar band at the marking. Cover the buttons in some of the spare silk, using four layers of fabric (see page 83 for instructions). Sew buttons to the left front and collar band at the markings.

PLANETS VEST

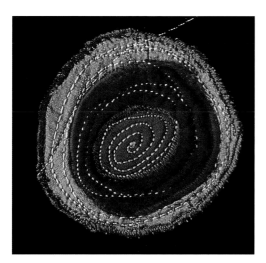

THIS VEST IS INSPIRED by old illustrations and maps depicting the stars, planets, and comets. The simple form of the circle embellished with stars and celestial symbols looks sumptuous in brightly colored silk. The black velvet base represents the denseness and darkness of space, on which the jewel-like colors positively shine out. The rings around the planets are stitched using metallic silver, gold, and copper threads, which represent the bright and shimmering stars. The overall effect is very dramatic and looks striking worn with a white shirt.

EQUIPMENT AND MATERIALS

Basic sewing kit (see page 124)

1¼yd (1m) black velvet

10in (25cm) double-sided
  fusible webbing

Small pieces of silk and velvet in
  assorted colors

Rayon threads to match fabric

Gold, silver, copper metallic threads

4 x ⅞in (22mm) self-cover buttons

Black silk thread

1¾yd (1.5m) red satin lining

28in (70cm) medium iron-on interfacing

Black cotton thread

1in (2.5cm) buckle

◆ *Enlarge the vest right front and left front templates by 279%. Enlarge the pocket welt templates by 226%. The button templates are shown actual size.*

1 Enlarge the pattern on page 137 as instructed. Measure in 10cm from all edges of the fabric. Mark with small dots, using tailor's chalk. Lay out the 1–Front and 6–Pocket welt pieces on the wrong side of the black velvet within the chalk dots. Using tailor's chalk, mark around the shape of both pattern pieces, remove the pattern, and then baste around the chalk line. Draw a ⅝in (1.5cm) seam allowance around the vest front outline with tailor's chalk. Turn the pattern pieces over to get the mirror image and repeat the marking on the velvet for the other side, leaving a 4in (10cm) space between the front pieces. Using the button template, draw five buttons on the velvet with tailor's chalk.

2 Enlarge the templates to the correct size and trace them using tracing paper and a pencil. Decide on the colors and fabric to be used for each circle. Draw all the circles (drawing a complete circle each time) for the vest

25¼in/62.8cm

13¼in/32.8cm

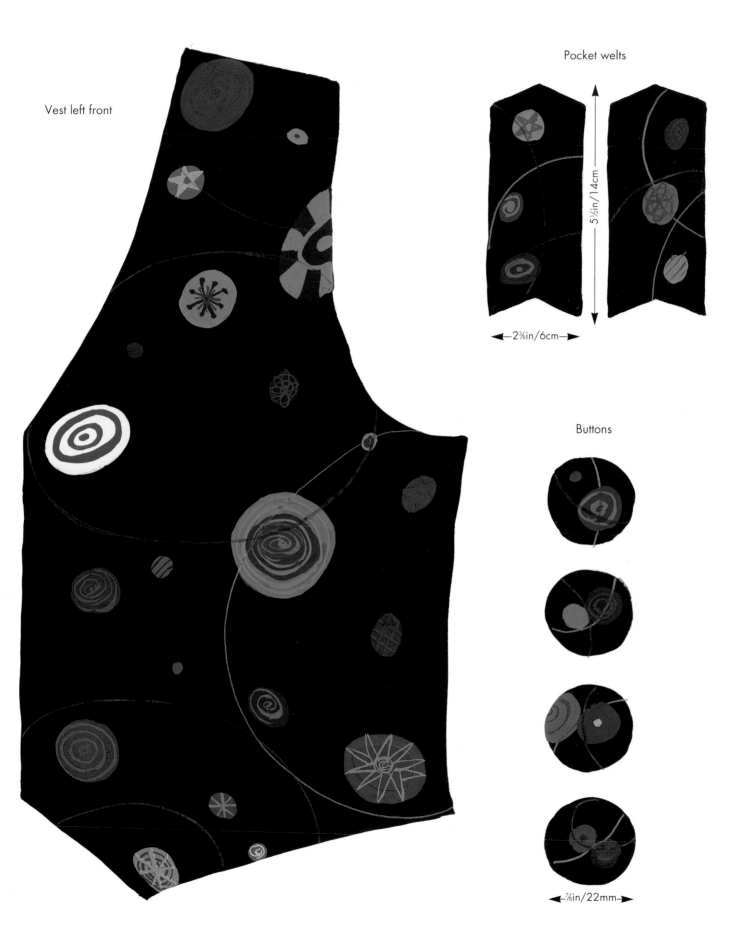

Vest left front

Pocket welts

5½in/14cm

←—2⅜in/6cm—→

Buttons

←—⅞in/22mm—→

fronts, pocket welts, and buttons onto fusible webbing, marking the right- and left-hand sides, and the color the circles will be, with a pencil. Cut out the circles roughly with scissors and fuse them onto the relevant-colored silk or velvet (see Basic Techniques, page 127). Cut out the shapes. Fuse them on top of the circles where indicated. Distribute the circles to their relevant place on the black velvet, remove the backing paper, and place them on the velvet following the design plan. Once you are pleased with the arrangement, fuse in position using the tip of the iron at a fairly high temperature and pressing gently around the shape. Take great care not to press too hard with the iron as this tends to mark or flatten the pile of the velvet.

3 Untighten an embroidery hoop to make it quite loose and then place it around a section of the velvet to be embroidered. Tighten the hoop, being careful not to make it too tight as this will mark the fabric. Referring to the design and color plan, embroider the circles on the fabric as follows:

Using rayon thread to match each circle of fabric, stitch around the circles in satin stitch, set at stitch width 3.

Using rayon thread in a contrasting color, fill in the shapes in the circles using running stitch as follows:

4 To embroider the spirals, start in the middle of the circle and embroider a solid dot by stitching a series of running-stitch circles in a spiral, close together. Then stitch a line, opening out in a spiral, to fill the space.

5 To embroider the concentric circles, start in the middle and embroider a small circle with two lines of running stitch. Leave a small gap,

then embroider another circle as before; repeat until the shape is filled.

To embroider concentric circles with a flower motif, repeat as above. Then, using the same-colored thread, start in the middle and stitch a curved line to the edge. Continue this curved line around and back to the middle to make a petal. Repeat eight times around the circle to make a flower.

6 To embroider an open-centered star, start at the bottom left-hand side of the circle and draw a five-pointed star. Fill in each point with rows of close running stitch, leaving a central, open pentagon (see diagram).

7 To embroider an icicle, start in the middle of the circle and stitch a small circle with two lines of running stitch. Stitch a line to the outer edge, then embroider a dot by working a series of circles in a spiral pattern, staying very close together.

Return to the middle of the circle and repeat the process eight times, moving around the circle, so that when you have finished it has been divided into eight equal segments.

Using a contrasting color of thread, repeat this process in the spaces in between each line of stitching. This time, take the line halfway toward the

outer edge of the circle and then return to the middle. Make sure that you do not stitch a dot (see the diagram).

8 To embroider the sun rays, start in the middle of the circle and embroider a small circle. Leave a gap, then repeat, embroidering a second small circle. Stitch lines radiating out in

the space between the second circle and the outer edge, and then fill in every alternate space with dense rows of stitching to create the sun rays.

9 To embroider the star flower, start in the middle of the circle and embroider a spiral. Stitch a line from the spiral to the outer edge of the circle, then take it back to the middle to make a triangle, making the petal of the star flower. Repeat as many times as you can to fit petals around the circle.

10 To embroider stripes, stitch two rows of running stitch in a vertical line across the circle, then leave a space and repeat to fill the circle. To embroider a geometric grid, repeat as above, stitching vertical rows of running stitch, then stitch on top with two rows of horizontal running stitch, the same width apart as the vertical lines.

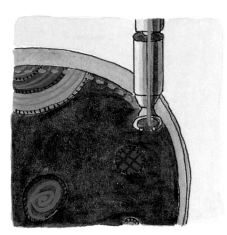

11 Rethread the sewing machine with metallic thread and, using a single row of running stitch, embroider five varying-sized circles onto each vest front and three curved lines across each pocket welt. To help achieve a well-shaped circle, you can use several different-sized embroidery hoops as guides, stitching a line following the outer edge of the hoop (see the diagram). Overlap the circles, and vary the colors of thread used.

12 To embroider the vest buttons, take the matching-colored thread for each circle and stitch around the edge in satin stitch, set at stitch width 3. Referring to the design plan, fill in the circles with either a dot or a spiral. Stitch across the buttons with single curved lines of metallic thread, using all the colors.

13 Remove the fabric from the embroidery hoop by loosening the screw and gently easing the fabric out (to help prevent marking the velvet). Press lightly on the wrong side of the velvet with a dry iron at a low heat. A hot iron will flatten the pile.

ASSEMBLY

This pattern makes a man's vest. (To make a woman's vest, use the pattern pieces given on page 138). Cut out the two embroidered 1-Front pieces, 6-Pocket welt pieces, and the buttons; make the buttons. Cut out the 3-Facing pieces from black velvet. Cut out pieces 1b, 2, 4, 5, and 7 from lining fabric, and then cut out pieces 3 and 6 from interfacing.

Fuse the interfacing to the wrong side of the 3-Front facings and 6-Pocket welts. Pin the 2-Back center pieces, right sides together. Stitch the pieces together with black cotton thread, ending 1.5cm (⅝in) up from the sloped edge. Press the seam open.

Fold the 5-Belt sections, right sides together. Stitch along the unnotched end and down the sides. Trim the seam, and clip the corners. Turn right side out and press with a warm iron. Baste the 5-Belt sections to the right side of the 2-Back center sections between the notches. Measure 2in (5cm) in from the edge and edge-stitch. Slip the buckle onto the left belt piece, to lie on the center back seam. Slipstitch the buckle into place.

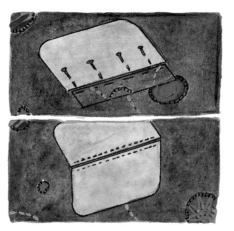

Pin the 4-Back side pieces to the 2-Back center pieces, with the right sides together. Stitch the two pieces together, then press open the seams.

To reinforce the pocket openings, cut two interfacing strips, with each measuring 1½ x 6⅜in (4 x 16cm). Iron these to the wrong side of the 1-Front pieces over the pocket markings. Fold the 6-Pocket welts, right sides together, and pin in position. Stitch the sides. Trim the seam, and clip corners diagonally. Turn right side out. Baste along the edge. Pin the welts to the right side of the fronts where marked, and baste in position. Pin the pouch pieces over and above each welt so that they meet, right sides together, and stitch (see the diagram). The upper stitching line should be ¼in (5mm) shorter than the lower one. Slash the fronts between these lines of stitching. Clip diagonally to each last stitch. Pull the pocket pouch pieces through the openings to the inside. Press the welts up over the openings, and stitch. Pin the 7-Pouch pieces together and stitch.

Pin together the 1-Front and 2-Back sides. Stitch, then press the seams open with a warm iron. To make the lining, stitch the 2-Back center seam and side seams, as for the vest. Press all the seams open with a warm iron. Pin 3-Facings to the 1b-Front facing edges, right sides together. Press the seams into the lining using a warm iron. Pin the completed lining to the vest, right sides together and seams matching. Stitch around outer edge. Stitch the neck and armhole edges to ¾in (2cm) from the shoulder seamlines. Trim the seams, clip the curves and trim corners diagonally.

Turn the vest right side out through one of the shoulder openings. Pin the vest fronts to the vest back, with right sides together at the shoulder seams, and stitch together. Turn in the shoulder allowances on the lining, and slipstitch the seams closed.

Machine-stitch four buttonholes into the left front, where they are marked. Then sew the buttons onto the right front, where they are marked.

SUNFLOWERS VEST

THIS SUMMERY VEST captures the intense color of sunflowers and is reminiscent of Spain and Italy, where there are fields full of these majestic giants. I was inspired to recreate the simple, abstract shapes of these after seeing a watercolor of sunflowers by the artist Friedensreich Hundertwasser. This vest uses the sunny colors of bright intense orange, yellow, and terracotta on linen and silk. The middles of the flowers are made from circles of different colors stitched on top to convey depth; the petals have frayed edges to give a rough texture. Compared to the size of the vest, the flowers are very large – and this helps to convey a feeling of dominance that is entirely in keeping with such enormous blooms.

EQUIPMENT AND MATERIALS

Basic sewing kit (see page 124)

1¾yd (1.5m) natural linen

Beige cotton thread

20in (50cm) double-sided fusible
   webbing

12in (30cm) each of copper, bright-
   orange, flame, coral-pink, pale-ocher,
   and golden-yellow silk

12in (30cm) each of terracotta and
   ocher linen

Assorted rayon threads to match fabric

4 x ⅞in (22mm) self-cover buttons

1¼yd (1m) green silk habutai lining fabric

28in (70cm) medium iron-on interfacing

1in (2.5cm) buckle

Oatmeal silk thread

◆ *Enlarge the templates by 273%*

1 Enlarge the pattern on page 138 as
   instructed. Measure in 10cm from
each edge and mark the central area
with dots, using tailor's chalk. Lay out
the 1-Front pattern piece on the wrong
side of the natural linen within the dots.
Using tailor's chalk, mark around the
shape and mark the darts. Remove the
pattern and baste around the line. Turn
the pattern piece over for the mirror
image and repeat marking for the other
side, leaving 10cm (4in) between the
fronts. of the vest. Pin center darts
together, and stitch with oatmeal cotton
thread. Press toward the sides.

2 Enlarge templates for the fronts and
   trace. Decide on fabric and colors
for each sunflower, looking at the
design and color plan on pages 32–3.
Draw the shapes onto fusible webbing,
and mark with a pencil the right- and
left-hand sides and color. Cut around
each shape and fuse to the relevant
fabric (see Basic Techniques page 127),
leaving ¾in (2cm) of fabric around the
shapes that have fringed edges.

TEMPLATE
Vest right front

24½in/61.7cm

13⅜in/33.6cm

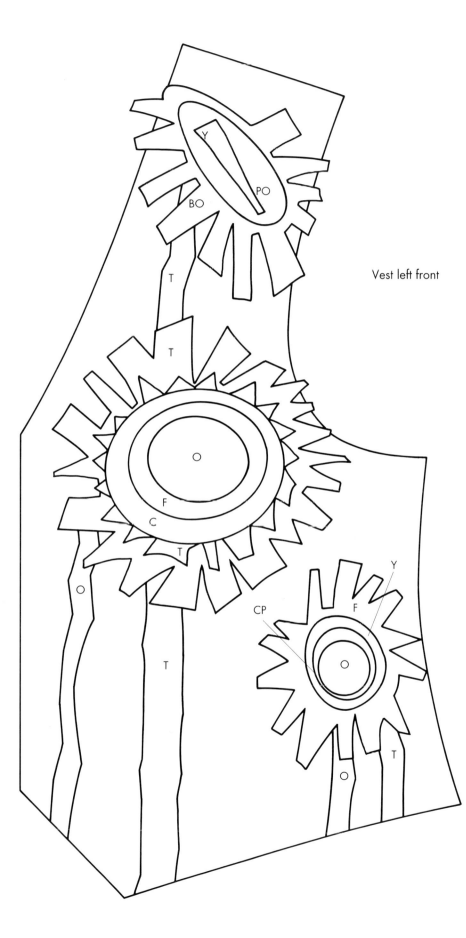

Vest left front

KEY

T	Terracotta linen
O	Ocher linen
C	Copper silk
BO	Bright-orange silk
F	Flame silk
CP	Coral-pink silk
PO	Pale-ocher silk
Y	Golden-yellow silk

3 Cut out the shapes. To make the fringed edges, pull out the side threads until you reach the fusible webbing; you may need to use a pin to separate the threads if you are having difficulties (see the diagram). Distribute the shapes to each side, remove the backing paper, and assemble the flowers, placing them on the linen vest front as indicated in the template. Once you are pleased with the arrangement of the sunflowers, fuse them into position.

4 Loosen the screw of an embroidery hoop and place the fabric in it. Then tighten the screw until the fabric is taut. Referring to the design and color plan on pages 32–3, embroider the sunflowers as follows:

Using the matching rayon thread for each color of fabric, embroider around each shape with five rows of running stitch. Then, using either a matching or contrasting rayon thread, fill in the

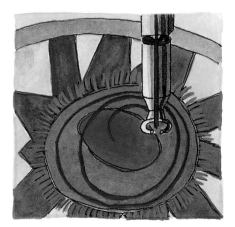

DESIGN AND
COLOR PLAN
Vest right front

shapes where indicated with either
continuous spirals or lines of running
stitch (see the diagram).

5 Embroider the stalks of the
sunflowers as follows:
Using a matching-colored rayon thread,
stitch around the stalk shapes using satin
stitch, set at stitch width 3.

6 Remove the fabric from the
embroidery hoop (see page 33).
Then press with a hot steam iron.

ASSEMBLY
This pattern makes a woman's vest (to
adapt the design for a man's vest, use
the pattern on page 137).

Cut out the two 1-Front pieces.
Draw one button on natural linen, two
on terracotta linen, and one on ocher
silk. Cut them out and assemble them.
Cut out pieces 2, 3, and 4 from natural
linen. Cut out pieces 1b and 2 from
lining fabric. Cut out piece 3 from
interfacing. Fuse the interfacing to the
wrong side of the 3-Front facings.

Pin the bust darts on the vest front.
Stitch, and press down to the armhole.
Fold the 4-Belts, with right sides
together. Stitch along the unnotched
end and down the sides. Trim the
seams, and clip the corners diagonally.
Turn right side out and press.

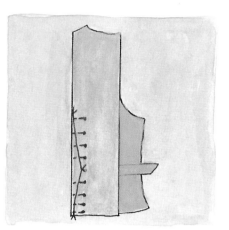

Vest left front

Pin the darts together on the 2-Back pieces. Place the 4-Belts on the right side of the back pieces inside the middle of the darts (see the diagram). Stitch and press the darts to the side. Slip the buckle onto the left belt piece, positioning it in the middle of the back piece. Slipstitch it into place.

Pin together the 1-Front and 2-Back sides. Stitch and press the seams open.

To make the lining, stitch the 2-Back, and 1b-Front facing darts, as for the vest. Pin the 3-Facings to the 1b-Front facing edges, with right sides together. Press the seams into the lining. Pin the sides together, and stitch. Press the seams open. Pin the lining to the vest, right sides together and seams matching. Stitch around the outer edge. Stitch both the neck and armhole edges up to ¾in (2cm) from the shoulder seamlines. Trim the seams, clip the curves and trim the corners.

Turn the vest right side out through one of the shoulder openings. Pin the vest fronts to the vest back, right sides together, at the shoulder seams, then stitch. Turn in the shoulder allowances on lining and slipstitch seams to close.

Make four buttonholes on the right front, where marked. Then, sew on buttons to the left front, using the oatmeal silk thread, where marked.

PATCHWORK VEST

THIS PATCHWORK VEST COMBINES the traditional technique of patchwork with vibrant, modern patterns applied and embroidered onto each individual square. The design is derived from the manipulation of basic forms and patterns. Circles, squares, diamonds, zigzags, waves, stripes, stars, spirals, and flowers are cut out from small pieces of silk and velvet in bold, bright colors, or stitched using vivid rayon threads. In total, the vest has nine different square designs and twelve different colored backgrounds. The squares are arranged randomly, but the designs and hues work together in harmony. The overall effect is a riotous explosion of color, shape, and texture.

Notice that even the buttons are covered with pieces of the patchwork squares – a

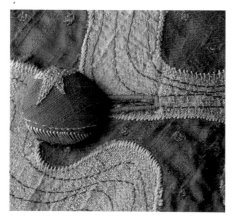

clever extra detail that helps to create an arresting and appealing blend of patterns.

EQUIPMENT AND MATERIALS
Basic sewing kit (see page 124)
4 x 4in (10 x 10cm) Cardboard
10in (25cm) each of black velvet and of
  deep-blue, purple, olive, dark-turquoise,
  bottle-green, red, ocher, lemon, dull-
  gold, burgundy, and black silk dupion

20in (50cm) double-sided fusible webbing
Small amounts of silk and velvet in
  assorted colors
Rayon threads in assorted colors
4 x ⅞in (22mm) self-cover buttons
28in (70cm) dark-turquoise silk dupion
1¾yd (1.5m) gold silk-satin lining fabric

28in (70cm) medium iron-on interfacing
Gold cotton sewing thread (for assembly)
1in (2.5cm) buckle
Dark-turquoise silk thread (for buttonholes)

KEY S Silk V Velvet
Shaded areas indicate fused-on fabric

TEMPLATES FOR PATCHWORK SQUARES

A

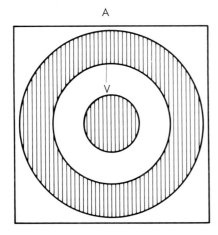

B

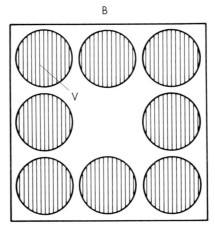

C

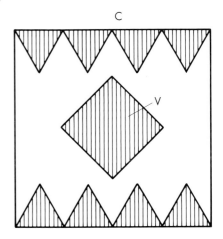

D

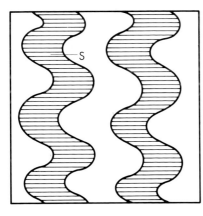

E

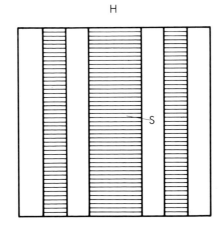

F

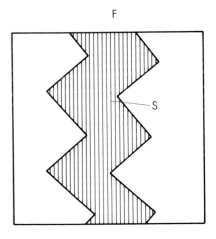

G

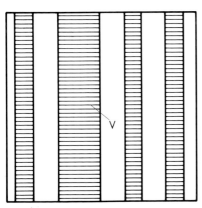

H

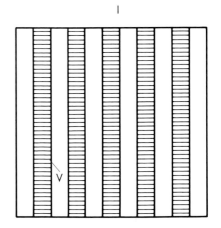

I

1 Make a cardboard template measuring 10 x 10cm (4 x 4in) for the squares. Lay the pieces of velvet and silk on a flat surface. Measure in 10cm (4in) from each edge and mark the central area with dots, using tailor's chalk. You will need 38 squares. Draw them out on the wrong side of each piece of fabric, within the chalk dots as follows:

Black velvet x 4	E
Deep-blue silk x 3	A C II
Purple silk x 4	A B D D
Olive silk x 4	A D I I
Dark-turquoise silk x 3	B D F
Bottle-green silk x 3	B D F
Red silk x 4	C F H H
Ocher silk x 4	D I I I
Lemon silk x 4	G
Dull-gold silk x 2	A H
Burgundy silk x 1	F
Black silk x 2	I

Baste around each chalk line and then draw a 1.5cm (⅝in) seam allowance around each square.

2 Following the templates, decide on the fabrics and choose the colors for each square. Draw all the shapes on fusible webbing, marking the color and the square with a pencil. Cut out the squares roughly and fuse them onto the relevant silk or velvet (see Basic Techniques page 127). Cut out all the shapes. Remove the backing paper, put the shapes on the squares and then fuse these in position.

3 Place the fabric in an embroidery hoop, making sure that it is taut. Following the design and color plan, embroider square A as follows:

Using matching thread, embroider around the velvet circles in satin stitch, set at stitch width 3. Embroider a spiral on the small circle, and three lines spaced evenly apart on the large circle,

using running stitch. Using a contrasting thread, stitch around the small circle, then embroider 28 lines radiating out to the large velvet circle, in running stitch. Stitch in each alternate section with densely packed vertical lines.

Using a second contrasting thread, stitch around the large velvet circle, then embroider 64 lines radiating out to the edges of the square, in running stitch. Fill in every alternate section with densely packed vertical lines.

4 Embroider square B as follows: Using a matching thread, embroider around all the velvet circles

with satin stitch, set at stitch width 3.

Using a contrasting thread, stitch three concentric circles onto the four velvet circles at each corner of the square, with three lines of running stitch. Stitch the outline of a 1⅜in x 1⅜in (3.5cm x 3.5cm) square in the middle. Divide this into four columns, and draw chevron shapes in each (see the diagram). Fill in each alternate chevron with densely packed vertical lines of stitching.

Using thread in a second contrasting color, embroider three concentric circles on the remaining velvet circles, as above. Fill in the remaining chevrons with densely packed vertical lines.

5 Embroider square C as follows: Using thread to match the color of the velvet triangles, embroider around the triangles with satin stitch, set at stitch width 3.

Using thread to match the color of the velvet square, embroider around the square with satin stitch, set at stitch width 3.

Using a contrasting thread, stitch rows of vertical lines spaced evenly apart onto the base silk in running stitch. Embroider around the velvet square close to the stitching above, using satin stitch set at stitch width 3.

Using thread in a second contrasting color, and starting in the middle of the square, embroider a small square and spiral out (within the square shape) until you fill the square, using satin stitch set at stitch width 2. Then embroider evenly spaced dots on top of the vertical lines. Embroider two concentric triangles on top of the velvet triangles, with a single line of stitching.

6 Embroider square D as follows: Using a thread to match the color of the silk waves, embroider around the waves in satin stitch, set at stitch width 3.

Using thread in a contrasting color, embroider on top of the silk waves, following the shape, with five lines of evenly spaced running stitch.

Using thread in a second contrasting color, embroider evenly spaced dots in the space remaining on the base silk, in running stitch.

7 Embroider square E as follows: Using thread in contrasting colors for each silk square, embroider around each square with several rows of running stitch. Divide each square into nine small boxes, and fill in five of the boxes with vertical and horizontal lines (see the diagram). In each velvet box, embroider the outline of a flower with two rows of stitching.

8 Embroider square F as follows: Using a contrasting thread, embroider around the silk zigzag with satin stitch, set at stitch width 4.

Using a second contrasting color, embroider a single line of running stitch (following the shape) in the middle of the silk zigzag. On the right edge of the silk zigzag, stitch a line next to the satin stitching above. In the spaces between the "V" shapes, embroider a spiral with a single line of stitching.

Using a third contrasting color, stitch a line on the left edge of the silk zigzag, next to the satin stitching above. Embroider a star in the spaces between the "V" shapes, and fill in with rows of running stitch close together.

9 Embroider square G as follows: Using a thread that is lighter in color than the base silk, embroider along the first and fourth velvet strip with satin stitch, set at stitch width 3. Using thread to match the velvet, embroider along the second velvet strip with satin stitch, set at stitch width 3.

Using a thread that is darker in color than the base silk, embroider along the third velvet strip with satin stitch, set at stitch width 3.

10 Embroider square H as follows: Using a thread to match the color of the large silk band, embroider along the band with satin stitch, set at stitch width 3.

Using thread to match the color of the two thin silk bands, embroider along both bands with satin stitch, set at stitch width 3.

Using thread in a contrasting color, embroider horizontal lines of evenly spaced running stitch across the square in the spaces between the bands. Fill the large band with evenly spaced embroidered dots.

Using thread in a second contrasting color, embroider a broken line of satin stitch, set at stitch width 1.5, down the middle of the two thin bands.

11 Embroider square I as follows: Using threads in a contrasting color, embroider around the first velvet strip with satin stitch, set at stitch width 2.5. In the space after the fourth velvet strip, embroider a single zigzag line in running stitch.

Using thread in a second contrasting color, embroider around the second velvet strip with satin stitch, set at stitch width 2.5. In the space before the first velvet strip, embroider a single zigzag line in running stitch. In the space after the fifth strip, embroider a vertical line down the middle, then small evenly spaced horizontal lines across the line.

Using the third contrasting color, embroider around the third velvet strip with satin stitch, set at stitch width 2.5. In the space after the first velvet strip, embroider a single vertical line of running stitch down the middle, then small evenly spaced horizontal lines across the line.

Using a fourth contrasting color, embroider around the fourth velvet strip with satin stitch, set at stitch

width 2.5. In the space after the second velvet strip, embroider a single wavy line in running stitch.

Using a fifth contrasting color, embroider around the fifth velvet strip with satin stitch, set at stitch width 2.5. In the space after the third velvet strip, embroider a single line of connecting embroidered spirals in running stitch.

12 Press all the pieces of fabric. Cut out the squares and, following the layout, distribute them on each side.

The vest is constructed in diagonal rows. Align the edge of the fabric with the presser foot and secure the start and end of stitching with a few stitches back and forth. Stitch the squares together in rows with cotton thread, as listed below. Press the seams open. Pin the rows together, matching all the seams. Stitch, then press the seams open.

Right side	Left side
Row 1: A I B D	Row 1: E F H I
Row 2: H E A D G	Row 2: D A B D G
Row 3: F B C E	Row 3: C A E C
Row 4: H I H F	Row 4: D I F I
Row 5: I G	Row 5: I G

13 Lay out the two sides of the vest. Enlarge the pattern on page 137 as instructed. Place the 1-Front pattern piece on top of the patchwork fabric so that you get a pleasing arrangement of the squares. Cut out both 1-Fronts. Cut out two 6-Pockets and four button templates in the remaining patchwork fabric. Make the buttons. Cut out two 3-Facings from the dark-turquoise silk dupion.

ASSEMBLY

Continue by following the instructions for making the Planets Vest, on page 27. This pattern makes a man's vest. To adapt the design for a woman's vest, use the pattern on page 138.

DESIGN AND COLOR PLAN

Pocket welt

5½in/14cm

2⅜in/6cm

25¼in/52.8cm

13¼in/32.8cm

Pocket welt

PATCHWORK LAYOUT

Row 2   Row 1

Row 4   Row 3

Row 5

Row 1
Row 2
Row 3   Row 4
Row 5

Buttons

⅞in/22mm

SPIRALS HAT

THE SIMPLICITY and charm of folk art, with its basic shapes, forms, and colors, is the inspiration for the design on the band of this velvet hat. Metallic threads are stitched onto a black velvet base, which enhances the simple design and gives it a luxurious quality. Thick copper thread is used for the large, irregular spiral shapes that dominate the hatband, while blue and red metallic threads are used for the hearts and flowers.

TEMPLATE / DESIGN AND COLOR PLAN

5½in/14cm

27¼in/68cm

EQUIPMENT AND MATERIALS
Basic sewing kit (see page 124)
1¼yd (1m) black velvet
Copper, red, and blue metallic
    textured threads
1¼yd (1m) stiffened iron-on interfacing
20in (50cm) black habutai silk lining
Black cotton sewing thread
24 x 1in (60 x 2.5cm) grosgrain
    ribbon

◆ Enlarge the template by 193%

1 Enlarge the pattern on page 139 as
instructed. Measure in 10cm (4in)
from each edge and mark the central
area with dots, using tailor's chalk. Pin
1–Side to the wrong side of the velvet
within the chalk dots and draw around
the shape with tailor's chalk. Remove
the pattern piece and baste around the

chalk line. Draw a ⅝in (1.5cm) seam
allowance around the piece. Enlarge the
template, measure the width of one of
the sections, and then mark each of the
eight sections on the velvet with a chalk
line (giving space for the spirals).

2 Place an embroidery hoop around
the velvet, taking care not to
tighten it too much. Referring to the
design and color plan, embroider the
fabric as follows, using running stitch:
Copper Stitch a double row of
stitching on the eight vertical lines.
Using two rows of stitching, embroider
a large spiral in each of the boxes,
reaching out to all the edges.
Red At the top of every alternate
vertical line, stitch the outline of a
heart, then fill it in to make solid.
Repeat the stitching and filling at the

bottom of every alternate vertical
plain line (these are the lines without
a heart at the top).
Blue At the top of all the remaining
vertical lines, stitch the outline of a
flower, then fill it in to make it solid.
Repeat at the bottom of all the
remaining lines (see the diagram).

3 Remove the fabric from the hoop, easing it out to prevent marking the velvet). Press lightly on the wrong side of the velvet with a dry iron set on low.

ASSEMBLY

Cut out pattern pieces 1, 2, and 3 from velvet and interfacing. Cut out pattern pieces 4 and 5 from lining fabric. Fuse the interfacing to the wrong side of the velvet sections.

To make the hat lining, fold over 4-Side lining, right sides together, to form a circle, and pin the back seam. Stitch with black cotton thread, then press open the seam. Pin the 5-Crown lining to the 4-Side lining, right sides together, making pleats evenly around the side lining until it fits (see the diagram). Stitch, then press the seam flat toward the crown.

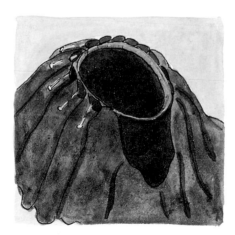

Fold the velvet 1-Side, right sides together, and pin the back seam. Stitch, then press the seam open. Clip the top (wider) edge at even intervals. Pin the 2-Crown to the 1-Side, right sides together, and ease into place. Stitch, and trim the seam allowance. Turn right side out. Slip the lining inside the

hat, and pin in place. Stitch ¼in (5mm) from the edge. Stitch the ends of both 3-Brim pieces together at the center back. Press the seam open. With right sides facing, pin the 3-Brim sections together. Stitch along the outer edge. Trim the seam allowance. Turn the 3-Brim right side out and finger press. Stitch the inner edges together ⅜in (1cm) in from the edge. Clip this edge at even intervals. Pin 3-Brim to the 1-Side, with the right side of 1–Side and the top side of 3–Brim together, and stitch. Finish the edge with overlocking or zigzag stitch.

Pin the grosgrain ribbon to the brim, folding over one end and overlapping the other end. Stitch along the same row of overlocking or zigzag stitching. Turn the seam and ribbon toward the crown of the hat.

NEHRU CAP

THIS CAP RADIATES the energy and vibrancy of a pattern seen on a marvelous, old-fashioned pinball machine. The simplicity of the Nehru-style cap is perfect for this lively design. The crown is embroidered with several stars within a large target, while the hatband has boxes with smaller starburst shapes inside, edged with a row of small dots on both top and bottom. The intensely colored silks add a rich quality to the embroidery.

EQUIPMENT AND MATERIALS

Basic sewing kit (see page 124)

24in (60cm) ocher silk dupion

20in (50cm) double-sided fusible webbing

8in (20cm) each of purple, turquoise,
    dark-green, violet, and cerise silk

8in (20cm) deep-red velvet

Small piece of deep-blue velvet

Purple, turquoise, deep-red, cerise,
    dark–green, violet, and deep-blue
    rayon threads

Ocher cotton sewing thread

10in (25m) Heavy iron-on interfacing

◆ *Enlarge the templates by 202%*

1 Enlarge the templates. Make four copies of the hatband template and join together widthwise. Using tailor's chalk, draw out two copies of the full-length hatband and two crowns on the ocher silk. Baste around the chalk lines. Draw a ⅝in (1.5cm) seam allowance. around the pieces.

2 Trace the circles, stars, and vertical bands shown on the template separately onto fusible webbing. Looking at the templates and the design and color plan, decide on the colors and fabrics for each, and mark these with a pencil. Cut out the shapes roughly and fuse onto the relevant fabric (see Basic Techniques page 127). Cut out the shapes. Fuse the crown's stars and the hatband's stars and circles on top of each other, as indicated. Remove the backing paper and place all the pieces onto the hatband and crown, following the template. Iron the pieces in place.

3 Place the fabric in an embroidery hoop so that it is taut. Embroider the crown as follows. Using matching thread for each star, outline the stars, or the points showing, in satin stitch, set at stitch width 3.

TEMPLATE FOR CROWN

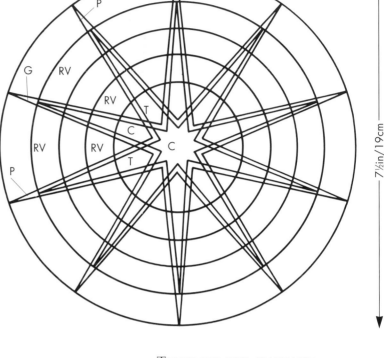

7½in/19cm

KEY

RV   Red Velvet
BV   Blue Velvet
T   Turquoise Silk
C   Cerise Silk
G   Green Silk
P   Purple Silk
V   Violet Silk

TEMPLATE FOR HATBAND

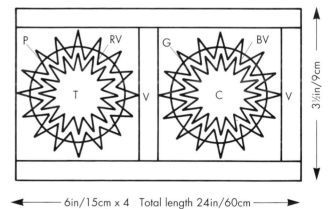

3½in/9cm

◀—— 6in/15cm x 4   Total length 24in/60cm ——▶

Turquoise Stitch the outline of a star in the middle of the cerise star in running stitch, then fill in the shape with stitching.

Deep red Stitch around the red velvet circles in satin stitch, set at stitch width 4. Embroider a dot in the middle of the turquoise star, using running stitch.

4 Embroider the hatband as follows. Using the matching thread for each circle, star, or band, outline each shape

in satin stitch, set at stitch width 3.

Turquoise Embroider a dot in the middle of the cerise stars, using running stitch.

Cerise Embroider a dot in the middle of the turquoise stars, in running stitch.

Dark green Stitch horizontal lines ¼in (7mm) apart across the violet silk bands using running stitch.

Violet Stitch a line across the upper and lower edges of the violet silk bands, along the whole length of the hatband,

DESIGN AND COLOR PLAN FOR HATBAND

DESIGN AND COLOR PLAN FOR CROWN

ASSEMBLY

Cut out the two crown and two hatband pieces. Cut out the interfacing pieces, and iron them to the wrong side of the lining crown and hatband.

Fold the hatband piece and pin the side edges together. Stitch with ocher cotton threads, and press the seam

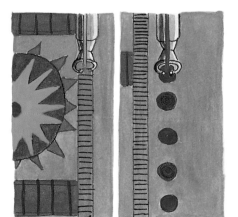

using satin stitch, set at stitch width 3. **Deep red** Embroider a row of large dots, ¾in (2cm) apart, in the space between the violet lines and the edges of the hatband, using running stitch. **Deep blue** Embroider a large dot in between each of the deep red dots above, using running stitch.

5 Remove the embroidered crown and hatband from the embroidery hoop and then press.

open. With right sides together, pin the hatband to the crown and stitch, snipping around the crown to ease the hatband in place. Fold under a ¼in (5mm) hem on the hatband lower edge. Turn right side out. Repeat for the lining pieces, but this time folding under a ⅜in (1.5cm) hem on the edge. Place the lining hat inside the silk hat, with wrong sides together. Turn under a ½in (1cm) hem to the inside and pin. Slipstitch the edge in place.

CHRYSANTHEMUM SCARF

THE BRIGHTLY COLORED, showy flower heads of chrysanthemums inspired the stitching on this scarf. For added exuberance, the florals are combined with stripes. There is a bold flower at each corner and one in the centre, which is framed with a striped turquoise border. For extra interest, the scarf is made with two different layers of chiffon – blue and fuchsia pink. Red and yellow flowers are embroidered onto both sides of the chiffon, which creates a reversible design that gives two completely different looks. The panels of the border are cut alternately to show both the blue and the pink chiffon.

EQUIPMENT AND MATERIALS

Basic sewing kit (see page 124)

1 x 1yd (90 x 90cm) fuchsia
silk chiffon

1 x 1yd (90 x 90cm) royal-blue
silk chiffon

Bright red, bright-yellow,
dull-red, dull-yellow,
turquoise and dull-orange
rayon threads

1 x ⅔yd (90 x 60cm) lightweight
cotton or muslin

Air/water-erasable marking pen

◆ *Enlarge the template by 726%*

1 Lay the piece of pink chiffon on a
flat surface, place the blue piece on
top, and pin together. Stitch ½in (1cm)
in from the outer edge using rayon
thread. Cut the cotton or muslin into
four strips, each measuring 36 x 6in
(90 x 15cm). Pin each strip around
the edges of the chiffon, and baste
together. For a border, you need to
embroider right to the edge of the
main fabric. Adding the cotton allows
you to do this and also prevents the
main fabric from puckering

2 Enlarge one of the templates to the
correct size. Lay the paper design
on a flat surface and tape down. Lay the
chiffon on top and pin it to the paper,

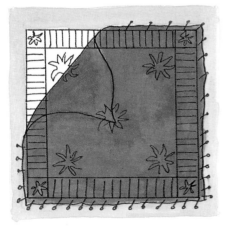

TEMPLATE / DESIGN AND COLOR PLAN

—36in/90cm sq—

matching all of the edges (see the
diagram). Using an erasable marking
pen, trace the design onto the chiffon
(see the design and color plan).
Untighten the screw of an embroidery
hoop to make it quite loose, and place
it around the chiffon, making sure that
both layers of fabric are flat. Tighten
the outer ring of the embroidery hoop,
taking care not to make it too tight as
this will mark the fabric. Before you
start embroidering the border, practice
the design on a spare piece of fabric to
get a feel for the amount of stitching
that is required to maintain a good
tension. Be careful not to make the
stitching too dense because this would
make the fabric very hard.

3 This scarf is designed to be seen
from both sides, so the back must
look as good as the front. Use the same
colored rayon thread in the bobbin as
on the top of the machine. It is a good
idea to fill a separate bobbin spool for
each color as this will save you time.
Embroider the chrysanthemums on the
scarf as follows:

Bright red or **bright yellow** Using
running stitch, stitch around the central
circle three times. Go around the inner
petal outline, and fill in the petal with
four rows of stitching (one row goes
from the middle to the tip of the petal,
then back to the middle).

Dull red or **dull yellow** Stitch around
the outer petal outline, and fill in the

TEMPLATE / DESIGN AND COLOR PLAN

reveal the pink in the stripes (see the diagram). Do not cut too close to the stitching as the fabric will start to come away, and be careful not to go through both layers of stitching. Go along the border of the two ends specified on

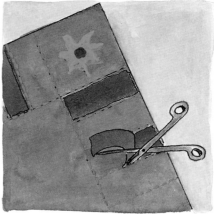

every alternate stripe. Turn the scarf over. To make the pink side facing, cut away the pink chiffon in the stripes of the two remaining borders to reveal the blue. Go along the border of the two ends, on every alternate stripe.

petal with five rows of stitching, as before (see the diagram).
Bright yellow or **bright red** Fill in the flower center with embroidered dots in a continuous spiral.

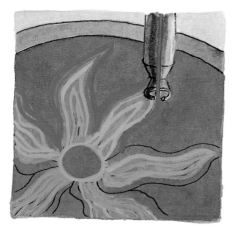

4 Embroider the border as follows:
Turquoise Stitch around the outer and inner edges, and all the short lines, using three rows of running stitch.

5 Embroider the scarf's corner boxes as follows:
Dull orange Stitch the outline of the central circle and fill in.
Dull yellow Stitch around the outline of the flower, and fill in with three rows of stitching.

6 Remove the scarf from the hoop. To make the blue side facing, use the border at the top and bottom of the scarf (opposite ends). Using small sharp scissors, cut away the blue chiffon to

7 Replace the fabric in the hoop and embroider as follows:
Turquoise Using satin stitch set at stitch width 3, stitch along the stripes, making sure that you cover all the cut ends of the chiffon. Stitch the inner line of the border, matching the lines.

8 Take the scarf out of the embroidery hoop. Remove the strips of cotton or muslin, then put the scarf back in the hoop. Stitch as follows:
Turquoise Using satin stitch set at stitch width 4, stitch slowly around the outer edge of the scarf to achieve a dense coverage and a smooth edge.

9 Remove the scarf from the embroidery hoop, then press on both sides with an iron.

IVY LEAVES SCARF

THIS SCARF RECREATES the wonderful sight of trees heavy with green leaves, with the sunlight filtering through. It is a lush forest that you can wear. The scarf is made from dark-green velvet, while the individual leaves have a bright-green silk backing. The colors stitched on the leaves represent all the different shades of leaves, moss, and bark that you can find in a wood. These are applied to the base, overlapping each other for a three-dimensional, textured quality. This design can be used just as successfully on vests and shawls – as well as scarves.

EQUIPMENT AND MATERIALS

Basic sewing kit (see page 124)

2¼yd (2m) dark green velvet

6 x 8¾in (15 x 22cm) cardboard

Forest-green, bottle-green, olive, dark-olive, dull-khaki, leaf-green, and biscuit rayon threads

Dark green/white, dark leaf-green/white shaded rayon threads

20in (50cm) green habutai silk

20in (50cm) double-sided fusible webbing

Green cotton thread

◆ *Enlarge the leaf templates by 135%*

1 Lay out the velvet fabric with the wrong side facing up. Measure 12in (30cm) in from one edge with a tape measure, and draw a line in tailor's chalk down the whole length of the fabric. Measure a further 12in (30cm) in from this chalked line, and draw

another line in tailor's chalk, as before. These are your scarf front and back pieces. Do not cut them out.

2 Trace the two templates in pencil. Make a cardboard template of each. Lay the remaining velvet, right side facing up, on a flat surface and draw around each template ten times with a chalk pencil to get ten large and small leaves for each end of the scarf.

3 Cut around the area with the drawn leaves, leaving enough fabric to fit the embroidery hoop. Before you start embroidering, make yourself a chart of how many leaves each color has. I used nine different threads, distributed as follows:

Forest green: A A B

Bottle green: A B

Olive: A B

Dark olive: A B

Dull khaki: A B B

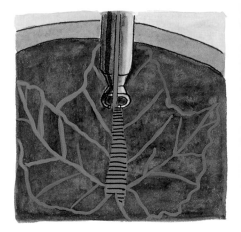

Leaf green: A B

Biscuit: A B

Dark green/white: A B

Dark leaf green/white: A B

4 Place one velvet leaf in a hoop. Using running stitch, stitch around the outline of the leaf. Then stitch the central stalk and main and minor veins. Using satin stitch set at stitch width 5, start at the top of the central stalk and

TEMPLATES

A

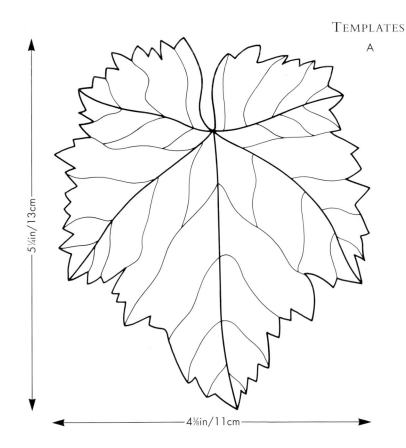

5⅛in/13cm

4⅜in/11cm

B

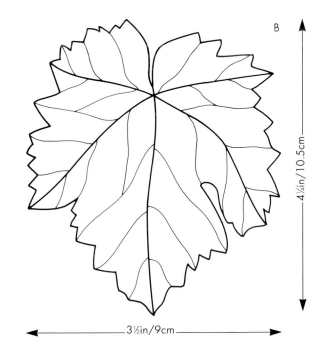

4⅛in/10.5cm

3½in/9cm

embroider a line tapering down to the tip of the leaf, ending in stitch width 0 (see the diagram). Repeat with the four main veins. Stitch around the outer edge of the leaf in satin stitch, set at stitch width 3. Change to running stitch and stitch a line around the leaf close to the satin stitch. Repeat for all 20 leaves.

5 Cut a piece each of habutai silk and fusible webbing the same size as the piece of velvet. Fuse the adhesive webbing onto the silk (see Basic Techniques page 127). Remove the backing paper and fuse onto the wrong side of the velvet. Using a sharp pair of scissors, cut out the leaves close to the single line of stitching.

6 Taking each leaf, and its corresponding colored thread, go around the outer edge slowly in satin stitch, set at stitch width 4, to give dense coverage and a neat, smooth edge. Repeat for all 20 leaves.

7 Lay the scarf front on a flat surface, right side facing up. Measure a ⅝in (1.5cm) seam allowance around all the edges, and mark with a line of pins. On each end, measure 13¾in (34.5cm) from the bottom, and mark with a line of pins. Distribute the leaves on each side of the front piece and overlap them as

DESIGN AND COLOR PLAN

12⅛in/30.5cm

10¾in/27cm

shown in the design and color plan. Move the leaves around until you are happy with the arrangement and the color balance. Pin in place.

8 Secure each leaf in position. Using thread the same color as the leaf, start stitching at the top of the central stalk, using satin stitch at stitch width 5. Embroider a line tapering down to the tip, ending in stitch width 0. In running stitch, stitch a line out to the tip on the two top main veins. Stop stitching just before the seam allowance on the leaves at the outer edges and bottom.

ASSEMBLY
Cut out the front and back pieces. Pin the leaves at the sides and bottom in toward the middle (to avoid sewing them into the seam). Place the back and front pieces right sides together. Stitch together, using green cotton thread, with a ⅝in (1.5cm) seam allowance. Leave a 4¾in (12cm) opening in the middle of one side. Trim and cut the corners. Turn the pieces right side out. Finger press the edges, and slipstitch the opening to close. Unpin the leaves, and open them out. Steam-press the scarf, being careful not to mark the velvet.

STARS AND SPIRALS BAG

THIS STARRY BAG takes its inspiration from old celestial maps and drawings of heavenly bodies. The simplicity of the ideas behind these illustrations is very appealing. This particular design is especially effective in its use of color, with star, circle, and spiral motifs repeated in different sizes to create the illusion of a starry night. Glowing silk shapes are placed on top of each other in a random pattern and positioned on a dark velvet base to allow the colors to shine.

TEMPLATE / DESIGN AND COLOR PLAN

10¼in/25.5cm

8¼in/20.5cm

EQUIPMENT AND MATERIALS

Basic sewing kit (see page 124)
20in (50cm) rich-blue velvet
10in (25cm) double-sided
   fusible webbing
Small pieces of silk in assorted colors
Rayon threads to match fabric
20in (50cm) navy habutai silk lining
Blue cotton thread
48in (1.2m) dusty-pink cord,
   ½in (1cm) thick

◆ *Enlarge the template by 117%*

1 Lay the velvet, wrong side facing up, on a flat surface. Measure in 4in (10cm) from one selvedge end and from the bottom, and mark the central area with dots, using tailor's chalk. Draw two pieces measuring 8¼ x 12⅛in (20.5 x 30.5cm) with tailor's chalk, within the dots, leaving 2⅜in (6cm) between each piece. Baste around the chalk line. Draw a ⅝in (1.5cm) seam allowance around both pieces.

2 Enlarge and then trace the template. Draw all the circles and stars for both sides of the bag on the fusible webbing. Cut out roughly and fuse onto the different-colored silks (see Basic Techniques page 127). Cut out the shapes. Fuse on top of the circles and stars where indicated. Distribute the shapes on each side of the bag; there should be eight large stars, eight small stars, and eight circles of various sizes for each side. Remove the backing paper and place the shapes on the velvet, following the design and color plan. Fuse in place using the tip of an iron at a fairly high temperature and pressing gently around the shape.

3 Untighten an embroidery hoop to make it quite loose and place it around the velvet. Tighten the hoop,

being careful not to make it too tight because this will mark the fabric. Embroider the circles as follows:

Using matching rayon thread, embroider around the edge of each circle with satin stitch at stitch width 3.

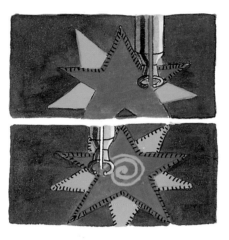

4 To embroider the top star, take the matching-colored thread and embroider around the edge with satin stitch, set at stitch width 3 (see the diagram). Change the thread color to that of the bottom star. Then, using running stitch, embroider the spirals. Start in the middle and embroider a solid dot, then stitch a series of circles opening out in a spiral pattern until you fill the space (see the diagram).

To embroider the bottom star, take the matching thread and embroider the five star points with satin stitch, set at stitch width 3.

5 Remove the fabric from the embroidery hoop by loosening the screw on the outer ring and gently easing the fabric out (this helps to prevent marking the velvet). Press lightly on the wrong side of the velvet with a dry iron at a low heat.

ASSEMBLY

Cut out the velvet back and front bag pieces. Cut out two pieces

8¼ x 11in (20.5 x 27.5cm) from lining fabric. Make a ⅝in (1.5cm) long cut on each side of the velvet back and front pieces 4in (10cm) down from the top. With the wrong side facing, turn under ⅜in (1cm) at the top edge, and ⅝in (1.5cm) at the sides above the cuts, and then press.

Turn down the top folded edge so that it meets the cuts. Using blue cotton thread, stitch close to the edge, ¾in (2cm) up from this line, to form a casing. Repeat for the other piece. Lay the two pieces together, right sides facing. Sew a ⅝in (1.5cm) seam around three sides. Turn right side out.

Lay the two lining pieces together, with right sides facing each other; stitch around the three sides. Turn under a ⅜in (1cm) hem, and press. Place the lining bag inside the velvet bag, wrong sides together. Slipstitch the top edge of the lining to the velvet casing

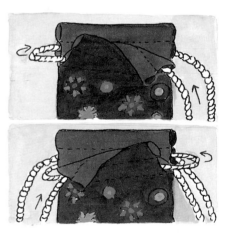

section. Cut the cord in half. Thread one cord through the front casing from right to left, then through the back casing from left to right (see the diagram). Knot the ends 2in (5cm) from the end. Thread the other cord through the casing the opposite way. Knot the ends 2in (5cm) from the end. Unravel the cords up to the knots and fray the ends.

SEA ANEMONES BAG

CORAL REEFS are teeming with strange and wonderful creatures in vivid and iridescent colors. One inhabitant is the sea anemone, the inspiration for this small bag. The design of the bag has a 1950s styling which combines well with the bright, bold imagery. The colors of the thick cotton and chenille threads – corals, pinks, and terracotta – come directly from these sea anemones, while the icy-blue background fabric captures the color of water. The overall feeling is fresh and modern.

EQUIPMENT AND MATERIALS
Basic sewing kit (see page 124)
20in (50cm) ice-blue silk dupion
4 x 12¾in (10 x 32cm) cardboard
Burnt-sienna cotton chenille thread
2 x terracotta, peach, coral, and saffron
    soft matte cotton embroidery thread
Terracotta, peach, coral, saffron,
    and ice-blue cotton sewing thread
8in (20cm) navy habutai silk lining
20in (50cm) heavyweight iron-on
    interfacing
48in (1.2m) piping cord,
    ½in (1cm) thick
1 x ⅝in (17mm) snap fastener

◆ *Enlarge the template by 142%*

1 Lay the silk dupion on a flat surface. Measure in 4in (10cm) from all edges, and mark the central area with dots, using tailor's chalk. Draw two squares 9 x 9in (22 x 22cm) with tailor's chalk, within the dots. Baste around the chalk line. Draw a ⅝in (1.5cm) seam allowance around both pieces. Enlarge the template and trace the large anemone shape and a circular outline for the small anemone. Make a cardboard template of each. On the wrong side of the fabric, draw nine anemones and 12 circles; position them as in the template, and mark the middle of each shape.

2 Place the fabric in an embroidery hoop, wrong side up, so that it is taut. For this design you will be using cable stitch (see Basic Techniques page 127). Wind the matte cotton embroidery thread, or the chenille thread, onto the bobbin. Place the bobbin in the case, and loosen the screw until you can fit the thread through the gap. Use a similar or matching-colored thin cotton thread on the top, and tighten the top tension.

Before you start embroidering the bag, practice the design on a spare piece of fabric, altering the top tension until you achieve a nice, smooth stitch.

3 Referring to the design and color plan, embroider the large anemones on the fabric, using different colors as indicated, as follows:
Burnt sienna, terracotta, or **peach**
Using running stitch and starting at the middle of the anemone, stitch around the outline of the anemone. Return to

the middle after each arm. Stitch another row inside the outline in the same way to fill in the shape of the sea anemone (see the diagram).

4 Embroider the small sea anemones, using different colors of thread as indicated in the plan, as follows:
Coral or **saffron** Using running stitch and starting at the outer edge of the circle, stitch a line toward the middle, stopping just before the middle, then return to the outer edge (see the diagram). The middle is to remain the base silk. Stitch right around the circle, back and forth.

5 Loosen the outer ring of the embroidery hoop and carefully remove the fabric, then press.

ASSEMBLY
Cut out the two embroidered pieces and the other pattern pieces from silk. Cut out the lining, the interfacing, and the 6-Base pieces. Fuse the interfacing to the wrong side of the 1-Front, 1-Back, 3-Facings, 2-Sides, and 5-Bottom fabric pieces.

Pin two 2-Side sections to the 1-Front, and stitch, using ice-blue cotton thread. Repeat for the 1-Back piece. Pin the 1-Front and 1-Back pieces, and stitch the sides together, ending at the small dot. Pin the 5-Bottom to the lower edges of 1-Front and 1-Back. Stitch, breaking at the small dots. Turn the bag right side out, creasing along the foldlines, and press.

To make the corded handle, cut the piping cord in half. With right sides together, fold the 4-Handle around half the length of the cord. Using a

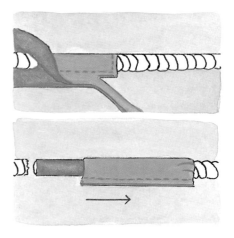

zipper foot, stitch across the end of the handle at the middle of the cord, making a ¼in (6mm) seam (see the diagram). Stitch close to the cord, stretching it slightly while you are stitching it, and trim.

To turn the 4-Handle piece right side out, pull out the enclosed cording. Trim the 4-Handle close to the stitching and cut the excess cording. Pin the handles to the upper edge of 1-Front

TEMPLATE / DESIGN AND COLOR PLAN

←————————10in/24.8cm sq————————→

and 1-Back, where marked, and baste in position. Stitch the snap fastener to the 3-Facings at the markings. Pin the 3-Facing sections together, and stitch the sides. Stitch the 1-Front and 1-Back lining sections together at the sides. Pin the 3-Facing to the upper edge of the 1-Lining, and

stitch. Trim, and press the seam toward the lining. Pin the 5-Bottom lining piece to the lower edges of the 1-Front and 1-Back pieces. Stitch, breaking at the small dots and leaving the back side open. Then, with right sides together, pin the lining to the bag, and stitch them together.

Turn the bag right side out through the opening in the lining. Slip the lining in place and press. Insert the 6-Base cardboard piece into the bag, through the opening in the lining. Pull the lining out and slipstitch the opening to close. Finally, slip the lining into its proper place.

CORAL BAG

THE THREE-DIMENSIONAL effect of stitching with elastic looks similar to pieces of coral on tropical reefs, hence the inspiration for this little velvet evening bag. The colors are taken straight from the source - pinks and grays, including a gray velvet shot with pink. The entire fabric is covered with stitched spirals, so that when the elastic is relaxed, the spirals stand out like little polyps. This really emphasizes the two colors of the shot fabric. The resulting bag is sumptuous, intriguing, and very tactile.

EQUIPMENT AND MATERIALS

Basic sewing kit (see page 124)

1⅜yd (1.2m) grey shot pink velvet

4 x 25yd (20m) reels of pink
   shirring elastic

Grey or purple rayon thread

12in (30cm) navy silk
   habutai lining

5½ x 5½in (14 x 14cm) medium-
   weight iron-on interfacing

Gray cotton thread

Strong thread

1⅜yd (1.2m) navy cording,
   ½in (1cm) thick

1 Lay the velvet on a flat surface,
with the wrong side up. In the
middle of the fabric, mark a rectangle
measuring 32⅜ x 13¼in (81 x 33cm)
with tailor's chalk (this is the area that
will be embroidered). Baste around
the chalk line.

Place the fabric in an embroidery
hoop, so that it is taut. Do not make
the hoop too tight as this will mark the
velvet. Wind the shirring elastic on the
bobbin (holding the elastic taut as you
wind). Place the bobbin in the case,
loosening the screw until you can fit
the thread through the gap. Use the
gray or purple rayon thread on the top.
Before you start embroidering, practice
working with the elastic (see Basic
Techniques page 127).

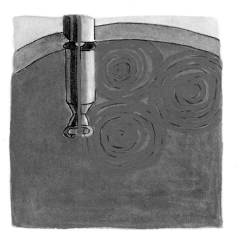

DESIGN AND COLOR PLAN

←————————————— 32⅜in/81cm —————————————

2 Using running stitch, embroider a
spiral, densely packed together at
the middle and opening out a little to
the sides (see the diagram). It should
have a circumference of 1¼in (3cm).
Cover the rectangle in spirals stitched
close together. When you remove the
hoop to embroider another section, the
fabric will contract (see the diagram),
making it difficult to place in the hoop,
so stretch the spare fabric out at each
side until taut, then tighten the screw.

3 Once you have covered the marked
area, remove the fabric from the
hoop. Steam-press it on both sides
(this will make the elastic contract even
more). The finished piece should
measure 6½ x 14¼in (16.5 x 35.5cm).

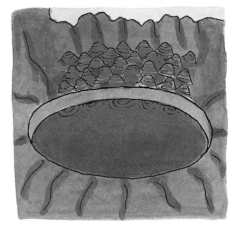

ASSEMBLY

Lay the velvet on a flat surface. Measure
7¼in (18cm) from the upper bag edge,
and draw a line. Measure 3in (7.5cm)
from the lower bag edge, and draw a
line. Measure a seam allowance of ⅝in

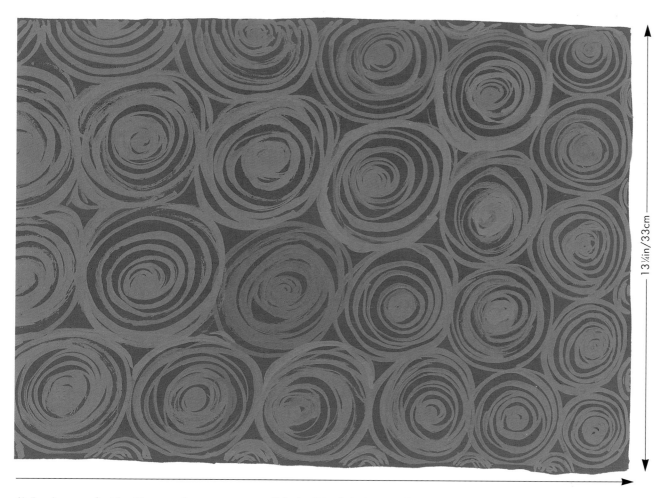

13¼in/33cm

(1.5cm) on each side. Cut out the piece. Cut out a piece measuring 1¼ x 7¼in (40.5 x 18cm) in the lining fabric. Draw a circle 4½in (11.5cm) in diameter. Cut out one each from lining fabric and interfacing. Fuse together.

Pin the sides of the lining section together, and stitch with gray cotton thread. Open out the seams, and press flat. Pin the bottom section to the lining bag section. Stitch, clipping around the seam allowance.

Pin the sides of the velvet section together, and stitch. Open out the seams, and press flat. Turn in a ½in (1cm) hem on the lower edge and stitch. Double a length of the strong thread and thread it through this hem. Pull as tight as possible (see the diagram). You should be left with a

small hole. Handstitch securely across the hole to close it. Turn the bag right side out. Place the lining bag inside the velvet bag, with the wrong sides together. Slipstitch the top edge of the lining to the velvet just above the elastic stitching. Turn in a ½in (1cm) hem on

the upper edge. Thread strong thread through this hem. Fold the upper edge down to the lining section. Pull the thread until this section fits the neck of the bag. Pin in place around the edge, encasing the lining, then slipstitch. Stitch a line 1in (2.5cm) in from the stitched edge (casing). Make a hole in the casing on each side, and stitch over the edges to prevent fraying.

Cut the cord in half. Thread the first cord through the front casing from right to left, then through the back casing from left to right. Knot the ends 2in (5cm) up from the end. Thread the second cord through the casing the opposite way. Knot the ends 2in (5cm) from the end. You should have a knot at each side. Unravel the cord up to the knot and fray the ends on both sides.

JEWEL PURSE

THE DEPTH AND THE INTENSITY of jewels in a setting of gold, silver, or enamel can be breathtaking. I was inspired by the shapes, colors, and quality of such jewelry to design something equally precious – and a little envelope purse for use with evening wear seemed ideal to embroider in this way. The design combines silk stripes, circles, and zigzags in intense colors, positioned on a luxurious red velvet background – and these are then further embellished with vibrant embroidery, sparkling metallic threads, and delicate beading.

EQUIPMENT AND MATERIALS

Basic sewing kit (see page 124)

16in (40cm) deep-red velvet

Small piece of blue chiffon

2¾ x 6¼in (7 x 15.5cm) double-sided fusible webbing

Small pieces of lilac, orange, and cerise silk

Cerise, orange, lilac, and deep-purple rayon threads

Gold, purple, and red metallic threads

Small orange beads

Long blue bugle beads

12in (30cm) black silk-satin lining fabric

Deep red cotton thread

1 x ⅝in (15mm) self-cover button

Deep-red embroidery thread

◆ *Enlarge the template by 201%*

1 Enlarge the template. Lay the velvet, wrong side facing up, on a flat surface. Measure in 4in (10cm) from one selvedge edge and 2⅜in (6cm) from the bottom, and mark the central area with dots, using tailor's chalk. Mark out a rectangle 6¼ x 10½in (15.5 x 26.5cm) with tailor's chalk, within the dots. Measure 8½in (21.5cm) up from the lower edge; mark at both sides. Draw a line from each point to the middle of the upper edge. Baste around the chalk line. Draw a ⅝in (1.5cm) seam allowance.

2 Trace the template. Cut out a piece of blue chiffon measuring 2¾ x 6¼in (7 x 15.5cm). Draw the shapes for the purse on fusible webbing, marking the color with a pencil. Cut out the shapes roughly and fuse them onto the relevant-colored silk (see Basic Techniques page 127). Cut out the shapes. Remove the backing paper and place the shapes on the velvet, following the design and color plan. Fuse in position using the tip of an iron

at a high temperature and pressing gently. Do not mark or flatten the pile of the velvet. Position the chiffon strip as indicated, and pin into place.

3 Place the velvet in an embroidery hoop. Embroider as follows:
Cerise Embroider around the edge of the stripes and diamond shape with satin stitch, set at stitch width 2.
Orange Embroider around the stripes and diamond shape with satin stitch, set at stitch width 2. Using running stitch, go around the edge of the blue chiffon. Stitch a zigzag line down the middle, then another in the opposite direction, to give a row of diamonds.
Lilac Stitch around the diamonds in a

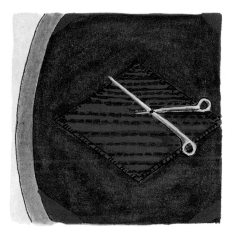

zigzag pattern using satin stitch set at stitch width 2, so that each diamond has either a lilac top or bottom. Stitch horizontal lines of running stitch across the cerise stripe, ⅛in (3mm) apart. Slash the fabric between the lines with sharp scissors (see the diagram).
Deep purple Embroider around the remaining edges of the diamonds, using satin stitch set at stitch width 2. The diamond will now have either a lilac top and deep purple bottom, or vice versa. Stitch horizontal lines of running stitch across the orange stripe and the diamond, ⅛in (3mm) apart. Slash the

fabric between the lines.
Metallic gold Stitch large running stitch dots around the cerise diamond. Stitch vertical lines, ⅛in (3mm) apart, in the velvet diamond, stitching two rows for each line. Embroider six circles, 1in (2.5cm) in diameter, on each side of the blue chiffon. Divide each alternate circle into six; fill in alternate sections with 12 rows of stitching. In between the silk stripes, embroider dots 1¼in (3cm) apart, following the plan.
Metallic purple Embroider continuous spirals on top of the cerise diamond in running stitch. In the spaces between the silk stripes, in between the gold dots, embroider solid diamonds, using satin stitch set at stitch width 0.5.
Metallic red Stitch horizontal lines of running stitch, ⅛in (3mm) apart, on the gold vertical lines in the velvet diamond, stitching two rows for each line. Divide the remaining circles on the chiffon into six; fill in alternate sections with 12 rows of stitching.

4 Thread lilac and deep purple rayon threads through the needle together. Set the sewing machine to stitch width 5 and stitch length 0.5. Using a tailor tacking foot, and with the feed dog teeth up, stitch a line down each end of the chiffon for a looped line (see the diagram). Remove the

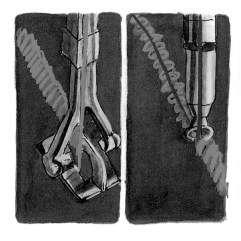

TEMPLATE

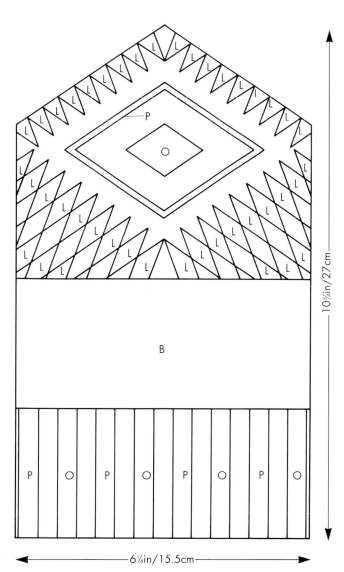

10¾in/27cm

6¼in/15.5cm

DESIGN AND COLOR PLAN

KEY
L Lilac Silk
P Pink Silk
O Orange Silk
B Blue Chiffon

tailor tacking foot, return the machine to freehand embroidery, and stitch a line down the middle of the chiffon to secure and flatten the looped stitches.

5 Handstitch five orange beads in a cluster in the middle of each metallic red circle, and three blue bugle beads in the middle of each gold circle.

6 Remove the fabric from the hoop. Press the velvet on the wrong side with a dry iron at a low heat.

ASSEMBLY
Cut out the embroidered shape. Cut out a piece the same size from lining fabric. Measure 5in (12.5cm) down from top edge of the velvet, and make a small cut on each side. Measure ¾in (2cm) up from the bottom edge, and make a small cut. Turn under a ¼in (5mm) hem, press and stitch.

With right sides together, fold the bottom edge up towards the top edge,

matching the cuts. Pin and stitch the sides with deep red cotton thread. Turn under a ⅝in (1.5cm) hem along the pointed edge. Press. Turn under a ½in (1cm) hem at the bottom (folded up) edge. Press. Turn right side out. Repeat for the lining piece. Place the lining inside the velvet purse, wrong sides together; pin and stitch the pointed edge. Fold the bottom edge hem to the inside. Slipstitch to the lining.

Cover the button with velvet (see page 83). Make a loop with doubled embroidery thread. Blanket stitch over to strengthen, then secure at the back.

71

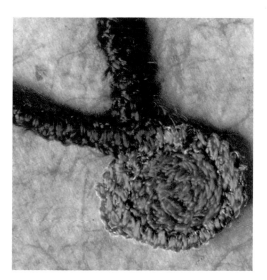

SPOTTED CHOKER

THIS CHOKER LINKS together the simple forms of triangles, circles, and squares in a continuous row. Coral reefs and tropical fish are the inspiration for the color of the piece, while chiffon and dissolvable fabric provide the base – and they have a wonderful affinity for each other. The chiffon triangles give the solidity needed for the main body of the choker, and these merge into delicate, stitched open triangles and light strands which hang beautifully around the neck.

TEMPLATE

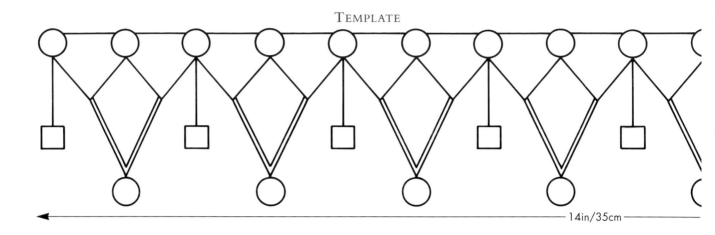

14in/35cm

EQUIPMENT AND MATERIALS
Basic sewing kit (see page 124)
20 x 10in (50 x 25cm) hot-water
  dissolvable fabric
16 x 1in (40 x 2.5cm) bottle-green
  silk chiffon
Turquoise, warm-red, and
  bright-orange rayon threads
1 x ¼in (7mm) nylon
  snap fastener

◆ The template is shown at actual size

1 Photocopy the template, which is
the size of the finished piece. Place
the paper pattern on a flat surface, and
tape the corners down with masking
tape. Place the hot-water dissolvable
fabric on top of the paper pattern, and
tape it securely to the surface, too.
(This means that neither piece can
move while you are tracing the design.)

Carefully trace the design of the choker
on the hot-water dissolvable fabric
using a sharp pencil.

2 Cut a strip of chiffon 1in (2.5cm)
wide and slightly longer than the
pattern piece. Pin it to the top line
of the choker. Place the fabric in an
embroidery hoop, making sure that
the design is straight. Before you start
embroidering the choker, practice
using the dissolvable fabric (see Basic
Techniques page 128).

3 Referring to the design and color
plan, below, start embroidering
the fabric, as follows:
Turquoise Using running stitch, stitch
a line along the top edge of the design
and the triangles. Remove the pins.
Remove the fabric from the
embroidery hoop and cut away the

chiffon close to the stitched line along
the triangles. Return the fabric to the
embroidery hoop. Using satin stitch set
at stitch width 2, embroider along the
top line of the chiffon. Using running
stitch, stitch around the outline of the
boxes, then fill them in with horizontal
and vertical lines to give a dense
coverage. Stitch around the outline
of the circles on the bottom edge with
four rows of stitching. Embroider on
top of these stitches with satin stitch,
set at stitch width 1.2.

4 Change to warm-red thread, and
embroider as follows:
Warm red Using running stitch, stitch
around the outline of the circles on the
top edge, then fill in with a densely
packed spiral. Stitch four lines from
the top circle diagonally across to the
bottom circle (see the diagram). Starting

DESIGN AND COLOR PLAN

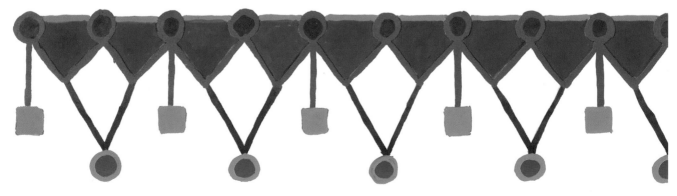

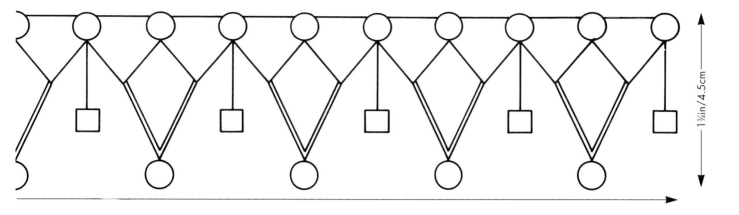

1¾in/4.5cm

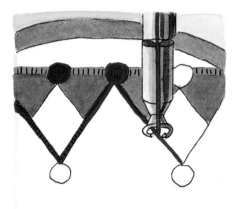

the red circles and the chiffon triangles. Embroider on top of all these shapes with satin stitch set at stitch width 1.5. Then stitch four lines of running stitch down the vertical lines, running from the red circles to the turquoise boxes. Embroider on top of all these lines with satin stitch, set at stitch width 1.5, making sure that you enclose all the

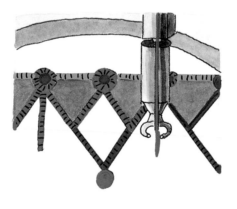

at the bottom tip of the chiffon triangles, embroider over these lines with satin stitch set at stitch width 1.5. Make sure that you enclose all the lines.

5 Change to bright-orange thread, and embroider as follows:
Bright orange Using running stitch, stitch a single line around the outline of

lines (see the diagram). Completely fill in the middle of the bottom circles, stitching first around and then across them, until they are densely filled.

6 When you have finished, check the stitching on the choker. Make sure that there are no loose stitches, and trim away any messy ends. Untighten the outer ring of the embroidery hoop and then carefully remove the fabric.

ASSEMBLY
Dissolve the fabric as directed (see Basic Techniques pages 128). When it is pliable and soft, it is ready. Leave the embroidery to dry flat. Once it is dry, press with a steam iron.

Handstitch the snap fastener securely to each end of the choker. Snap together to complete the piece.

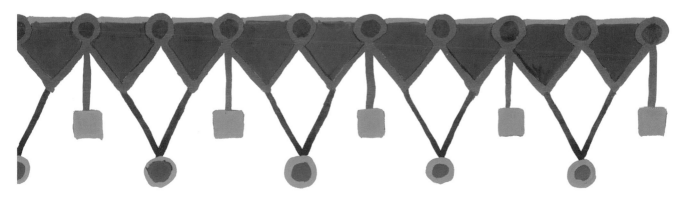

ELEGANT EARRINGS

THE FORMS, PATTERNS, and colors of Anglo-Saxon and Roman jewelry inspired these embroidered pieces. Jewelry has to be structurally sound, but it can also be delicate and exquisite. The lacy effect achieved using dissolvable fabric allows you to execute a design that, when dissolved, is composed entirely of stitching. The filigree drop earrings use a limited palette of sophisticated coloring. The long, delicate strands, like the tentacles of a Portuguese man-of-war, add elegance and a wonderful flowing motion. The design of the triangular earrings is an intriguing composition of boxes, dots, and triangles. Rich colors echo the vibrancy and intensity of gemstones and jewels, and contrast with the delicate, lacy quality of the stitching.

FILIGREE EARRINGS

EQUIPMENT AND MATERIALS

Basic sewing kit (see page 124)

10 x 10in (25 x 25cm) hot-water dissolvable fabric

Deep-purple, shocking-pink, and bright-blue rayon threads

Adhesive

2 x earring backs and butterflies

◆ *The template is shown actual size*

1 Photocopy the template, which is shown at the correct size. Place it on a flat surface, and tape it down. Place the hot-water dissolvable fabric on top; tape it to the surface to make sure that neither piece moves while tracing. Trace the design on the hot-water dissolvable fabric with a pencil.

2 Place the fabric in an embroidery hoop, ensuring that the design is straight. Before starting, practice using the dissolvable fabric (see Basic Techniques pages 128).

3 Referring to the design and color plan, embroider the earrings as follows, using running stitch only:

Deep purple Stitch around the outline of the earring. Fill in the upper and two lower boxes with horizontal and vertical rows of stitching to give a dense coverage. Embroider the five vertical lines with four vertical rows of stitching each. Catch them together all the way up the length with horizontal rows of stitching.

Shocking pink Embroider a horizontal line through the middle of the second box with three rows of stitching. Stitch equally spaced vertical lines along the second and third boxes. Embroider a zigzag line down the length of one of the short vertical lines.

At the bottom, fill in the three circles, going around and then across, until they are densely filled. Stitch back up on the zigzag line. Repeat on the other two short lengths.

Bright blue In the space between the second and third box, embroider three dots, going around and then across, until they are densely filled. Make sure that you stitch them to the upper and lower edges. Stitch a horizontal line on top of the deep purple stitching, at the top and bottom of the circles. Embroider a zigzag line down the length of the remaining vertical lines. At the bottom, fill in the two diamonds, going around and then across, until they are densely filled. Stitch back up the line on top of the zigzag line (see the diagram).

4 Embroider the other earring in the same way. When you have finished, check the stitching on both.

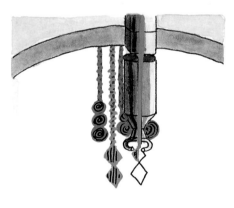

Make sure that there are no loose stitches, and trim off any messy ends. Remove the fabric from the embroidery hoop.

ASSEMBLY

Dissolve the fabric as directed (see Basic Techniques pages 128). When pliable and soft, it is ready. Leave to dry flat.

TEMPLATE   DESIGN AND COLOR PLAN

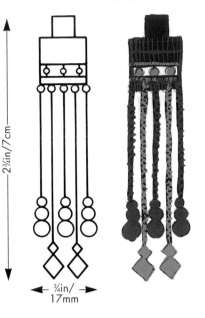

2¾in/7cm

¾in/ 17mm

Once dry, press with a steam iron. Glue the earring backs to the wrong side of the earrings at the upper box. Leave to dry, then attach the butterflies.

TRIANGLE EARRINGS

EQUIPMENT AND MATERIALS

Basic sewing kit (see page 124)

10 x 10in (25 x 25cm) hot-water dissolvable fabric

Golden-yellow, deep-purple, bright-blue, and shocking-pink rayon threads

Adhesive

2 x earring backs and butterflies

◆ *The template is shown actual size*

1 Photocopy the template, which is the size of the finished piece. Place the template on a flat surface, and tape it securely with masking tape. Place the hot-water dissolvable fabric on top, and tape it to the surface (to make sure that neither piece moves while you trace the design). Trace the design on the dissolvable fabric using a sharp pencil.

TEMPLATE

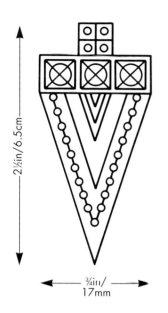

2½in/6.5cm

¾in/17mm

DESIGN AND COLOR PLAN

2 Place the fabric in an embroidery hoop, making sure that the design is straight. Practice using the dissolvable fabric as directed (see Basic Techniques pages 128). Once you feel confident, start on the earrings.

3 Referring to the design and color plan, embroider with running stitch except where specified, as follows:
Golden yellow Stitch around the outline of the earring. Fill in the upper box with horizontal and vertical lines to give a dense coverage. Stitch around the outline of the three lower boxes with four rows of stitching, then stitch across these with horizontal rows of stitching to bind them. Stitch the outline of the bottom triangle with four rows of stitching. Embroider over the four rows with satin stitch, set at stitch width 1, trapping all the lines.
Deep purple Stitch around the outline of the upper yellow box three times. Divide the box into four, using three rows of stitching. Go to the boxes below. In the central box, embroider a dot, going around and then across until

it is densely filled. Stitch the outline of the inner triangle with four rows of stitching. Stitch across these with horizontal rows to bind them.
Bright blue In the top left upper yellow box, embroider a dot. Stitch diagonally across to the bottom right-hand side, and embroider another dot. Go to the lower right-hand box, and embroider a dot, going around and then across, until it is densely filled. Embroider a row of continuous spirals and dots in the space between the yellow and purple triangles (see the diagram). On the bottom yellow line

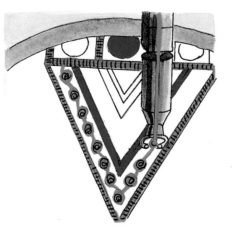

of the lower boxes, stitch a zigzag line across with two rows of stitching.
Shocking pink In the spaces left in the upper yellow box, embroider a dot, as with the blue. Go to the lower boxes and embroider a dot in the remaining box, going around and then across, until it is densely filled. On the top yellow line of the lower box, stitch a zigzag line across with two rows of stitching. Fill in the inner triangle with horizontal and vertical lines of stitching, to give a dense coverage.
Golden yellow Embroider a small "V" in the pink stitched triangle with four rows of stitching. In the lower box, embroider a cross on top of the circles, from the top line to the bottom line, with two rows of stitching.
Deep purple Starting at the top of the outer triangle, embroider a zigzag line across the yellow and blue stitching to the purple line, down to the tip and back up to finish at the other side, using two rows of stitching. Embroider a single-line small triangle inside the small yellow "V".

4 Embroider the second earring in the same way. When you have finished, check the stitching on both earrings. Make sure that there are no loose stitches, and trim any messy ends. Loosen the outer ring of the embroidery hoop and then carefully remove the fabric.

ASSEMBLY
Dissolve the fabric as directed (see Basic Techniques pages 128). When it is pliable and soft, it is ready. Leave to dry flat. Once dry, press the embroidery carefully with a steam iron.

Glue one earring back to the wrong side of each of the earrings at the upper box and then leave to dry. Finally, attach the butterflies.

BUTTONS

BUTTONS ARE AN IMPORTANT feature in a garment. They add the vital finishing touch which, if not considered, can upset the overall balance of the design. These buttons are embroidered in an assortment of designs and sizes, using silk and velvet. The images are taken from many sources: flowers, the sun, stars, and Celtic crosses, as well as simple structures and shapes such as grids, targets, checkerboards, quarters, concentric circles, diamonds, and chevrons. All the shapes are appliquéd or embroidered onto the base fabric.

EQUIPMENT AND MATERIALS

Basic sewing kit (see page 124)

8 x 8in (20 x 20cm) double-sided
  fusible webbing

Small pieces of silk dupion in
  assorted colors

Small pieces of velvet, as above

Rayon threads to match fabrics

⅞in (22mm), ¾in (19mm) and
  ⅝in (15mm) self-cover
  buttons

◆ *Reduce the templates by 50%*

1 Reduce the templates to the correct size and trace them. Draw all the shapes on fusible webbing, marking the colors and button with a pencil. Cut out the shapes and fuse onto the relevant-colored silk or velvet (see Basic Techniques page 127). Cut out the shapes. Distribute the shapes on each button, remove the backing paper, and place the shapes on the relevant-colored silk or velvet, following the design and color plan. Fuse the shapes into position.

2 To embroider the ⅞in (22mm) starburst button, draw around the button template on deep-blue velvet using tailor's chalk. Place a golden yellow silk starburst on the circle, center it, and fuse. Place the fabric in a hoop and stitch as follows:

Golden yellow Embroider around the starburst in running stitch. Stitch a line down the middle of all the points; embroider the edge of half of the points with three rows of stitching.

Turquoise From the middle, stitch a line of satin stitch, set at stitch width 2, on the other side of the points.

3 To embroider the ⅞in (22mm) Celtic cross button, draw around the button template on deep-red velvet using tailor's chalk. Place a deep-turquoise silk cross on the circle, center it, and fuse in position. Place the fabric in a hoop and stitch as follows:

Dark purple Embroider around the cross in satin stitch, stitch width 2.5.

Leaf green Embroider a line inside the purple line in satin stitch, set at stitch width 2.

Golden yellow Stitch a small cross in the middle, using a single line of running stitch.

4 To embroider the ⅞in (22mm) grid button, draw around the button template on golden-yellow silk dupion using tailor's chalk. Place dark-blue silk strips across the circle; fuse in position. Place terracotta silk strips across the circle; fuse in position. Place the fabric in a hoop; stitch as follows:

Terracotta Embroider around the terracotta strips in satin stitch, set at stitch width 2.

Dark blue Embroider around the dark blue strips in satin stitch, set at stitch width 2, stitching on top of the terracotta strips (see the diagram).

TEMPLATES / DESIGN AND COLOR PLAN

◄─── ⅞in/22mm ───►   ◄─── ¾in/19mm ───►   ◄─── ⅝in/15mm ───►

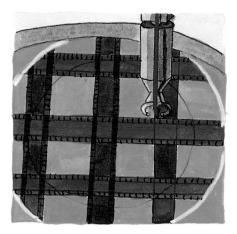

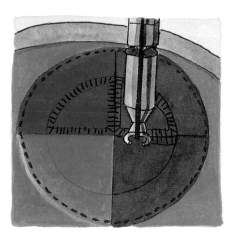

width 3. Stitch eight lines radiating out from the diamond, with four rows of running stitch in each (see the diagram). **Warm red** Using two rows of running stitch, first embroider a line from each point of the diamond into the middle, then finish with a dot.

5 To embroider the ⅜in (19mm) sun button, draw around the button template on violet silk dupion using tailor's chalk. Place a pale-blue silk circle on the circle, center it, and fuse in position. Place the fabric in a hoop and stitch as follows:
Pale blue Embroider around the circle in satin stitch, set at stitch width 2. Then stitch a circle in the middle of the remaining space using three rows of running stitch.
Golden yellow Embroider a dot in the middle. Stitch around the blue silk circle, then embroider lines radiating out to the edge. These should be the thickness of eight rows of stitching.

6 To embroider the ⅜in (19mm) target button, draw around the button template on grayish-pink velvet using tailor's chalk. Place turquoise, orange, and silver silk circles on the circle, and fuse in position. Place the fabric in an embroidery hoop and stitch as follows:
Turquoise Embroider around the turquoise silk circle in satin stitch, set at stitch width 2.5.
Orange Embroider around both edges of the orange and silver silk circles in satin stitch, set at stitch width 2.5.
Turquoise Embroider a running stitch dot in the middle of the silver circle.

7 To embroider the ⅞in (19mm) quarters button, draw around the button template on deep-purple silk dupion using tailor's chalk. Place burgundy, scarlet, and pale-blue silk quarters on the circle, and fuse in position. Place the fabric in an embroidery hoop. Using a matching rayon thread, embroider around each colored segment in satin stitch, set at stitch width 2.5 (see the diagram).

8 To embroider the ⅝in (15mm) diamond button, draw around the button template on deep-blue velvet using tailor's chalk. Place a golden-yellow silk diamond on the circle, center it, and fuse in position. Place the fabric in a hoop and stitch as follows:
Golden yellow Embroider around the diamond in satin stitch, set at stitch

9 To embroider the ⅝in (15mm) flower button, draw around the button template on golden-yellow silk dupion using tailor's chalk. Place a burgundy silk flower shape on the circle, and fuse in position. Place the fabric in a hoop and stitch as follows: Using a matching rayon thread, embroider around the flower in satin stitch, set at stitch width 2.5.
Orange Leave a space, then stitch a flower shape, following the shape of the fused-on silk flower, using four rows of running stitch.

10 To embroider the ⅝in (15mm) chevron button, draw around the button template on deep-green silk dupion using tailor's chalk. Place a beige silk chevron on the circle then fuse in position. Place the fabric in a hoop and stitch as follows:
Beige Embroider around the chevron in satin stitch, set at stitch width 2.
Red Stitch a line down the middle of the silk chevron, using running stitch. following the shape. Embroider a dot in the space above the chevron.

ASSEMBLY
Cut out each circle of fabric and, with the wrong side facing up, place a button in the middle. Working your way around the edge, fold the ends in, and attach them to the prongs of the button. Turn the button over halfway around to make sure that the design is centered. Position the back plate on top of the button back and snap in place.

HOME FURNISHINGS

SILK PATCHWORK QUILT

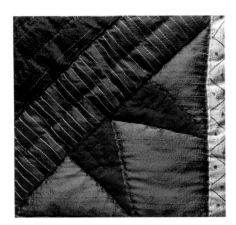

THE TRADITIONAL PATTERNS and motifs of American patchwork quilts, and the technique of patchwork itself – sewing small pieces of fabric together to form a continuous geometric surface – inspired this design. For the patchwork squares, I used designs incorporating the simple shapes of honeycombs, stars, squares, triangles, and diamonds. The shapes are cut from brightly colored silk and appliquéd onto a subtly-shaded silk base, then embellished with vibrant stitching. In total, there are six designs for the squares, on six different background colors. The patchwork is constructed in diagonal rows, with the designs and colors of the squares working together in symmetry. A two-colored striped border, with starburst squares at each corner, provides a strong frame for the main panel. The finished spread is a lustrous combination of colors, patterns, and textures.

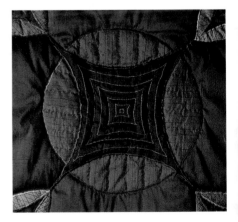

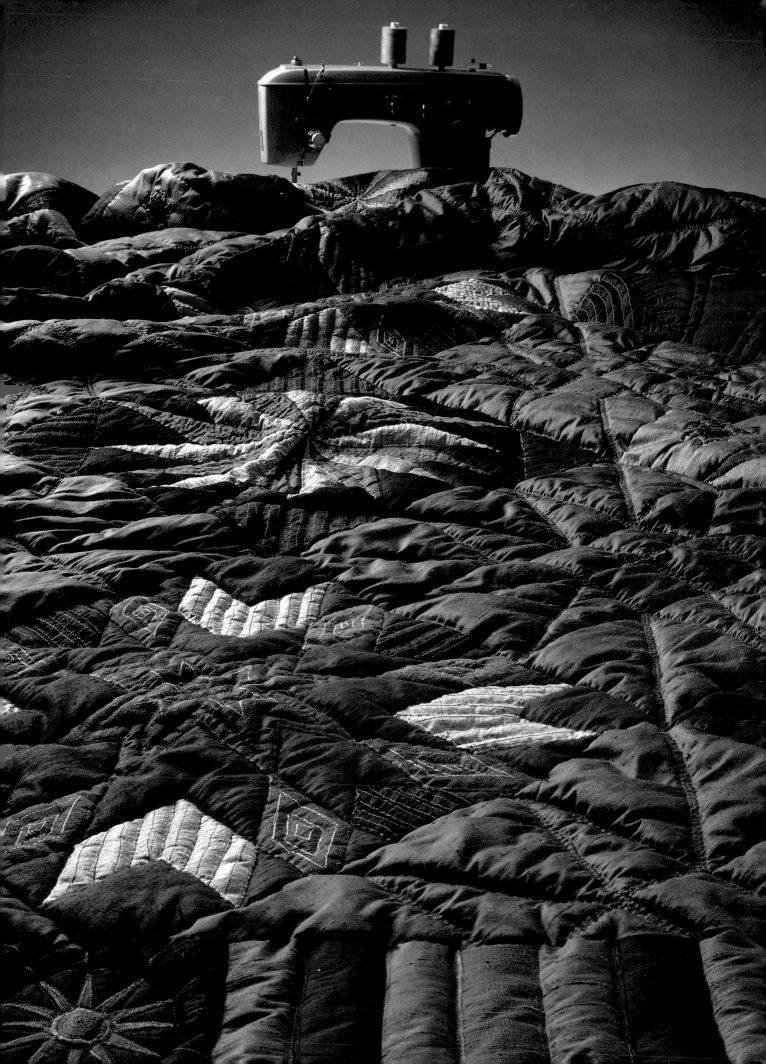

EQUIPMENT AND MATERIALS

Basic sewing kit (see page 124)
13½yd (12m) ocher silk dupion
26 x 26in (65 x 65cm) cardboard
1¼yd (1m) each of pale blue-gray, deep-purple, bright-blue, burgundy, pink, and terracotta silk dupion
1¼yd (1m) double-sided fusible webbing
Small amounts each of violet, turquoise green, ice-blue, cerise, dark-green, pale-peach, and silvery-green silk dupion
Burgundy, pink, deep-purple, bright-blue, turquoise-green, violet, ice-blue, terracotta, cerise, peach, dark-green, silvery-green, pale blue-gray, and ocher rayon threads
82 x 103in (204 x 257cm) batting
4 x terracotta quilting thread

◆ *Enlarge the templates for the appliquéd squares by 421% and those for the corner squares by 410%. The quilt is made up of 12 plain and 12 appliquéd squares, 17in (42.5cm) square. The finished quilt measures 81 x 102in (202.5 x 255cm).*

1 Lay the ocher silk on a flat surface and cut out the following pieces; a ⅝in (1.5cm) seam allowance is included:

For the quilt back: cut two pieces measuring 41¼ x 102in (103 x 255cm). For the plain squares: cut 12 squares measuring 18¼ x 18¼in (45.5 x 45.5cm). Cut five of the squares in half diagonally to give the side triangles, and cut one square in quarters diagonally to give the corner triangles. For the binding: cut a length 14⅜in (36cm).

2 For the 12 appliquéd squares, make a cardboard template 18¼ x 18¼in (45.5 x 45.5cm). Lay out the different-colored silks. Measure in 4in (10cm) from all edges. Using tailor's chalk, mark the central areas with dots, then draw two squares on each piece of silk, within the dots, allowing 2⅜in (6cm) between each square. Baste around the chalk lines. For the border squares, make a cardboard template 6¾ x 6¾in (16 x 16cm). Measure in and mark 4in (10cm) from each edge, and draw eight small squares on the deep-purple silk, within the dots. Baste around the line.

3 Enlarge the templates for the appliquéd squares. Decide on the colors and fabric for each square, referring to the templates and to the design and color plan. Draw all the shapes on fusible webbing, marking with a pencil the color and the square. Cut out the shapes and fuse them onto the relevant silk (see Basic Techniques pages 127). Cut out the shapes . Remove the backing paper and place them on the squares. Fuse in position.

4 Lay out the rest of the ocher silk. For the border, measure in 4in (10cm) from one side and the top. Using tailor's chalk, mark the central area with dots and draw four strips 33¾ x 6¾in (84.5 x 16cm) and four strips 33¾ x 6¾in (111 x 16cm) within the dots. Baste around the chalk line. Draw 96 strips 33¾ x 6¾in (4 x 16cm) on fusible webbing. Fuse 48 of the strips to the burgundy silk, and 48 to the pale blue-gray silk. Cut them out and remove the backing paper. Following the plan, place the strips, spaced 1½in (4cm) apart and alternating the colors, on the border. Fuse in position.

5 Start with the blue-gray appliquéd square, place the fabric in a hoop, so that it is taut. Following the template and design plan, embroider as follows:
Burgundy Embroider around three edges (leaving the bottom right edge) of the same-colored silk diamond with satin stitch, set at stitch width 3. Stitch a star around the top left and bottom right deep-purple silk stars, ¼in (5mm) away, with two rows of running stitch.
Pink Embroider around the three remaining edges of the same-colored silk diamonds with satin stitch, set at stitch width 3. Stitch around the remaining purple silk stars, ¼in (5mm) away, with two rows of running stitch. Embroider a circle in the middle of the purple stars, filling this in with a densely packed spiral, using running stitch.
Deep purple Embroider around the edge of the same-colored silk stars with satin stitch, set at stitch width 2. Stitch four concentric diamonds onto the pink silk diamonds using two rows of running stitch.
Bright blue Stitch four concentric diamonds on the burgundy diamonds, using two rows of running stitch.

6 Embroider the deep-purple appliquéd square as follows:
Turquoise green Embroider around two edges (leaving the short inner edge) of the same-colored silk triangle with satin stitch, set at stitch width 3. Stitch vertical lines on top of the violet silk triangles, ¼in (5mm) apart, using a single line of running stitch.
Violet Embroider around the edges of the same-colored silk triangles with satin stitch, set at stitch width 3. Stitch horizontal lines on top of the ice-blue

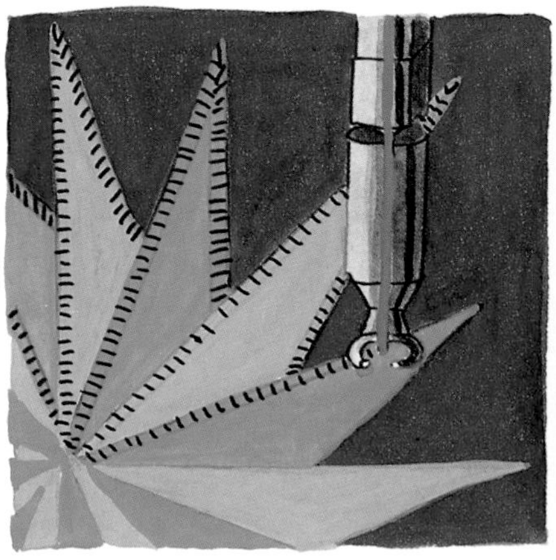

TEMPLATE FOR BLUE-GRAY SQUARE

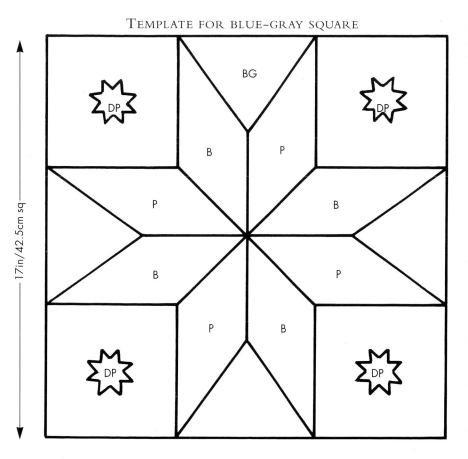

17in/42.5cm sq

TEMPLATE FOR DEEP-PURPLE SQUARE

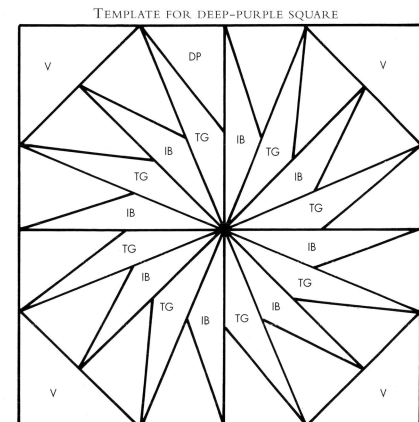

17in/42.5cm sq

silk triangles, ¼in (5mm) apart, using a single line of running stitch.

Ice blue Embroider around the two remaining edges of the same-colored silk triangles with satin stitch, at stitch width 3 (see the diagram).

Terracotta Stitch three concentric triangles on the turquoise triangles.

7 Embroider the bright-blue appliquéd square as follows:

Ice blue Embroider around the edges of the same-colored silk triangles and long, thin silk strips with satin stitch, set at stitch width 3. Stitch two concentric triangles on the terracotta triangles, using two rows of running stitch. Stitch vertical lines on top of the terracotta strips, ¼in (5mm) apart, using a single line of running stitch. Embroider a zigzag line down the long purple strips using two rows of running stitch.

Deep purple Embroider around the top edges of the same-colored silk triangles and both edges of the long thin silk strips with satin stitch, set at stitch width 3. Stitch two concentric triangles on top of the cerise silk triangles, using two rows of running stitch. Stitch vertical lines on top of the cerise silk strips, ¼in (5mm) apart, using a single line of running stitch. Stitch a zigzag line down the long ice-blue silk strips using two rows of running stitch.

Cerise Embroider around the three edges of the same-colored silk strips and two edges of the triangles (not the bottom edge) with satin stitch, set at

KEY

BG Pale blue-gray silk
B   Burgundy silk
P   Pink silk
DP   Deep-purple silk
V   Violet silk
TG   Turquoise-green silk
IB   Ice-blue silk

stitch width 3. Embroider dots in between the zigzag line down the long deep-purple silk strip using running stitch. In the central square, embroider a small box in the middle, fill it in with densely packed running stitch, then embroider three concentric squares, ¾in (2cm) apart, using two rows of running stitch.

Terracotta Embroider around the top edges of the same-colored silk strips and two edges of the triangles (not the bottom edge) with satin stitch, set at stitch width 3. Embroider dots in between the zigzag line down the long ice-blue silk strips using running stitch. In the central square, embroider three concentric squares in between the cerise-colored concentric squares, using two rows of running stitch.

8 Embroider the burgundy appliquéd square as follows:

Peach Embroider around the edges of the same-colored silk star with satin stitch, set at stitch width 3. Stitch seven concentric quarter-circles on top of the green silk quarter-starbursts, using a single line of running stitch.

Terracotta Embroider around the edges of the same-colored silk circle with satin stitch, set at stitch width 3. Stitch a star on top of the peach silk star, ⅝in (1.5cm) in from the edge,

KEY

BB	Bright-blue silk
IB	Ice-blue silk
T	Terracotta silk
C	Cerise silk
DP	Deep-purple silk
B	Burgundy silk
G	Dark-green silk
PP	Pale-peach silk
P	Pink silk
SG	Silvery-green silk
BG	Pale blue-gray silk

TEMPLATE FOR BRIGHT-BLUE SQUARE

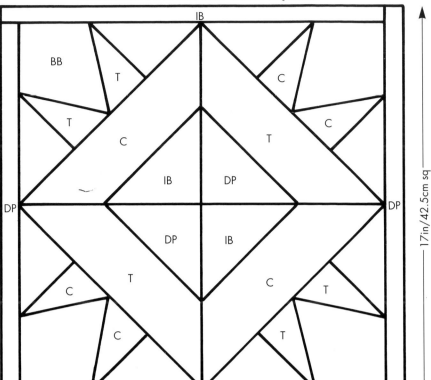

17in/42.5cm sq

TEMPLATE FOR BURGUNDY SQUARE

17in/42.5cm sq

TEMPLATE FOR PINK SQUARE

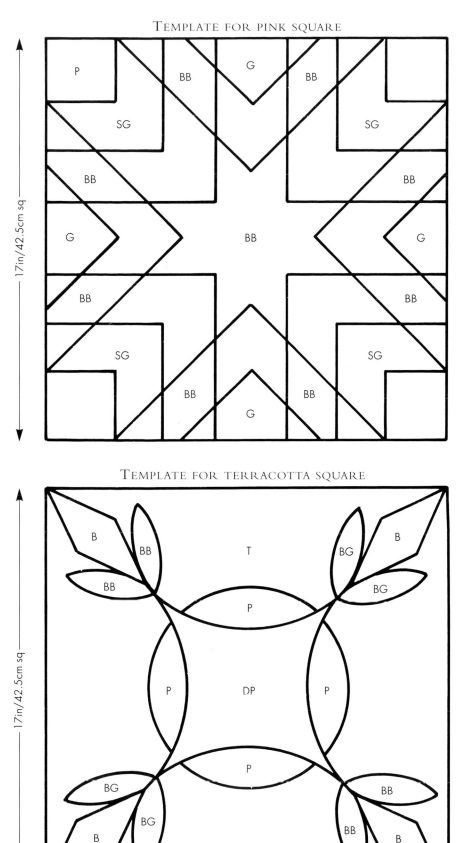

17in/42.5cm sq

TEMPLATE FOR TERRACOTTA SQUARE

17in/42.5cm sq

using two rows of running stitch.

Pink Embroider a star on top of the peach silk star, ½in (1cm) in from the terracotta stitched star, using two rows of running stitch.

Dark green Embroider around the edges of the same-colored silk quarter-starbursts with satin stitch, set at stitch width 3. Stitch two concentric quarter-circles, ¼in (5mm) away from the green starburst points, ⅝in (1.5cm) apart, using a single line of running stitch. Fill the terracotta circle with a spiral, starting in the middle with a dot. Embroider a star on top of the peach silk star, ¼in (5mm) in from the pink stitched star (starting from the terracotta circle), using one line of running stitch.

Cerise Embroider a star on top of the peach silk star, ¼in (5mm) in from the green stitched star, using two rows of stitching. Fill in each of the points with two "V" shapes, using a single line of stitching for each. Stitch three concentric quarter-circles, starting at the green starburst points, ⅝in (1.5cm) apart (in between the green lines), using a single line of stitching.

9 Embroider the pink appliquéd square as follows:

Bright blue Embroider around the edges of the same-colored silk star and diamonds with satin stitch, set at stitch width 3. Stitch vertical lines on top of the green silk pieces, ¼in (5mm) apart, using a single line of running stitch.

TEMPLATE FOR DEEP-PURPLE BORDER SQUARES

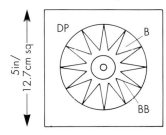

5in/12.7cm sq

Dark green Embroider around the edges of the same-colored silk pieces with satin stitch, set at stitch width 3. Stitch vertical lines on top of the silvery-green silk chevrons, ¼in (5mm) apart, using a single line of running stitch. Starting ½in (1cm) in from the edge of the blue silk star, embroider two concentric stars 1¼in (3cm) apart, using two rows of running stitch.

Silvery green Embroider around the edges of the same-colored silk chevrons with satin stitch, set at stitch width 3. Fill in the blue silk diamonds with three concentric diamonds using two rows of running stitch. Embroider a star on top of the blue silk star, in between the green stitched stars, using two rows of running stitch.

Terracotta Embroider a square in the middle of the blue silk star and divide it into quarters with four rows of running stitch.

Pink Embroider an "M" shape on the four sides of the terracotta square, using two rows of running stitch.

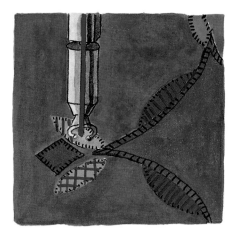

10 Embroider the terracotta appliquéd square as follows:
Deep purple Embroider around the edges of the same-colored silk curved-edged square with satin stitch, set at stitch width 3. Fill in the bright-blue and pale blue-gray leaves with a trellis

pattern, using a single running stitch (see the diagram).

Bright blue Embroider around the edges of the same-colored silk leaves with satin stitch, set at stitch width 3. Fill the deep-purple curved-edged square with six concentric curved-edged squares, using a single line of running stitch.

Pale blue-gray Embroider around the edges of the same-colored silk leaves with satin stitch, set at stitch width 3.

Pink Embroider around the edges of the same-colored silk circle with satin stitch, set at stitch width 3. Fill in the burgundy diamonds with two concentric diamonds, using satin stitch set at stitch width 2.

Burgundy Embroider around the edges of the same-colored silk diamonds with satin stitch, set at stitch width 3.

11 Embroider the deep-purple appliquéd squares for the corners of the border as follows:
Burgundy Embroider around the edge of the same-colored silk circle with satin stitch, set at stitch width 3.
Bright blue Embroider around the edges of the same-colored silk star with satin stitch, set at stitch width 3. Then stitch a line from each of the points of the star out to the edge of the square, with a single line of running stitch.
Ocher Embroider around the edges of the same-colored silk circle with satin stitch, set at stitch width 3.
Deep purple Fill in the middle of the ocher circle with a spiral using a single line of running stitch.

12 Embroider the four sides of the border as follows:
Burgundy Embroider around the

edges of the same-colored silk strips with satin stitch, set at stitch width 3.
Bright blue Embroider around the edges of the same-colored silk strips with satin stitch, set at stitch width 3.

13 Press all the completed patchwork squares, the border strips and all the ocher pieces with an iron. Cut the pieces out and arrange in their appropriate positions, following the design and color plan.

ASSEMBLY

Continue as follows, referring also, for more detailed instructions on how to quilt, to the Basic Techniques section, page 131. The quilt is constructed in diagonal rows. Stitch the plain and patchwork squares together in rows and press the seams open with an iron. Pin the rows together, making sure that you match the seams carefully. Then stitch the rows together, and press the seams open.

Construct the border following the design and color plan. Pin and stitch the corner squares to the longer side pieces. Pin the border's short top and bottom edges to the quilt and stitch. Pin the border's longer side edges to the quilt and stitch in place.

Pin the quilt back sections together along the long edges, stitch, and press the seam allowance to one side. Steam-press the quilt front and back. Place the quilt back, wrong side up, on a large flat surface, smoothing it flat. Secure it in place with masking tape. Place the batting carefully on top of the quilt back, matching all edges. Place the patchwork quilt top, with the right side facing up, over the batting, smoothing all three layers into place.

Baste the layers together, working from the middle out to the edges, horizontally, vertically, and diagonally across the quilt. Stitch four rows of concentric basting to hold the three layers together securely.

QUILTING

You can quilt either by machine or by hand (follow the instructions given for both in Basic Techniques page 131). Whichever method you use, it is advisable to use a large quilting hoop or frame to help you maintain an even tension throughout the fabric.

Place the quilt in the hoop. Quilt around the outline of all the squares. For the appliquéd squares, quilt around the outline of all the individual shapes. Stitch the centers of the appliquéd squares as follows:

Pale blue-gray square Working from the outer edge inward, quilt around the first and third concentric pink and

burgundy diamonds. Then quilt along the pink stitching around the deep purple star.

Deep-purple square Quilt the second concentric triangle in each turquoise green triangle. Quilt every third vertical line in each violet triangle.

Bright-blue square Quilt the third and sixth concentric squares in the ice-

blue/deep-purple square. Quilt a concentric square in the middle of the cerise and orange square. Quilt the second concentric triangle in each of the cerise and orange triangles (see the diagram).

Burgundy square Quilt the first and second concentric stars in the peach star. Quilt the second, fourth, and sixth concentric quarter-circles, and second and third cerise stitched concentric quarter-circles in the green starbursts.

Pink square Quilt the first and third concentric star in the blue star. Quilt the second concentric diamond in each blue diamond. Quilt every second vertical line in the silvery-green chevrons and green arrows.

Terracotta square Quilt around the second, fourth, and sixth concentric squares in the deep-purple curved square. Quilt the first concentric diamond in the burgundy diamond. Quilt every third vertical line in the pink circle.

For the plain squares, follow the quilting plan to fill in the stitching pattern, working two or three rows of stitching where indicated.

For the border, stitch along the two longer edges of each colored strip. Quilt around both of the circles and the starburst on the appliquéd squares at each corner. Then trim away any excess fabric or batting to make a clean edge. The border should measure 5¼in (13cm) wide.

BINDING THE QUILT

Using the 14⅜in (36cm) piece of ocher silk allocated (the full width of the fabric), cut nine strips 1½in (4cm) wide. Sew these together widthwise, to measure 41ft 8in (10.25m). Bind the quilt, following the instructions for binding edges that are given in Basic Techniques page 132.

QUILTING PLAN FOR PLAIN SQUARES

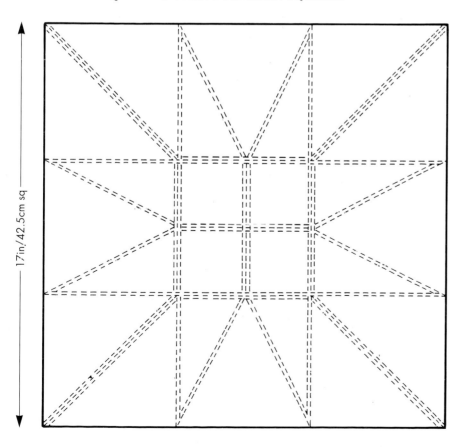

17in./42.5cm sq

SOLAR PILLOW

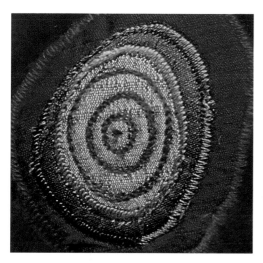

ASTROLOGY, THE SKY, STARS, planets, and other celestial objects provided the inspiration for this delightful pillow. Deep-red velvet, representing the denseness and darkness of space, was used for the base, on which the brightly colored shapes glow. The circles are decorated with varied symbols derived from illustrations – and the addition of random yellow dots embroidered around the circles creates the impression of a starry sky. One side of the pillow is elaborately decorated, while the other has only a single, central motif surrounded by yellow dots.

EQUIPMENT AND MATERIALS
Basic sewing kit (see page 124)
28in (70cm) deep-red velvet
8in (20cm) double-sided fusible webbing
Small pieces of silk and velvet in
    assorted colors
Rayon threads in assorted colors
Red cotton sewing thread
14in (35cm) zipper
18 x 18in (45 x 45cm) pillow form

◆ *Enlarge the template by 251%*

1 Enlarge the pillow template. Lay the velvet on a flat surface. Measure in 4in (10cm) from one side and the bottom edge. Using tailor's chalk, mark the central area with dots, then draw two squares measuring 18 x 18in (45 x 45cm) within the dots. Baste around the chalk line. Draw a ⅝in (1.5cm) seam allowance around both squares.

2 Trace the template. Draw all the circles for the pillow front on fusible webbing (note that some motifs have smaller circles fused onto larger ones). For the pillow back, draw out another of the blue circles motif shown in the middle of the pillow front onto fusible webbing. Mark the front and back pieces and the color with a pencil. Cut out the shapes roughly and fuse them to the relevant silk or velvet (see Basic Techniques page 127). Cut out the shapes. Fuse the circles on top of circles where indicated. Remove the backing paper, and place the circles on the velvet, following the design and color plan. Fuse in position, with the tip of an iron at a fairly high temperature and press gently around the shape.

3 Untighten an embroidery hoop to make it quite loose and place it around the velvet. Tighten the hoop,

being careful not to mark the fabric. Embroider the circles as follows. Using matching thread, go around each circle in satin stitch, set at stitch width 3. In the circles with patterns, use a contrasting thread and fill in the shapes with running stitch, as follows:

4 To embroider the spirals, stitch a solid dot in the middle (by stitching a series of close circles in a spiral pattern). Then stitch a line opening out in a spiral, until the space is filled, using three to five rows of stitching.

5 To embroider the concentric circles, start in the middle and embroider a small circle, using six rows of running stitch. Leave a small gap, then embroider another circle as before, repeating until the circle is filled.

6 To embroider the flower, start in the middle and stitch a curved line out to the edge. Continue this curved line around the other side and back to

the middle to make a petal, using three rows of running stitch for each petal (see the diagram). Repeat eight times.

7 To embroider the icicle, start in the middle and stitch a line to the outer edge, then embroider a dot. Return to

the middle and repeat this eight times. Using a different-colored thread, repeat in the spaces in between, this time taking the line only half way before returning to the middle.

8 To embroider the propeller, stitch a line across the circle from one side to the other. Stitch six lines (12 segments), filling in every alternate segment with rows of stitching packed densely together (see the diagram).

9 To embroider the coral, start at the edge of the circle and embroider a line that curves into and away from the

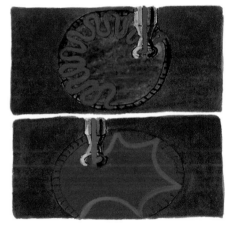

middle in a coral shape (see the diagram) using two rows of running stitch. Embroider a dot in the middle.

10 To embroider the cell, start at the edge of the circle and embroider a cell shape (see the diagram) using four rows of running stitch. Embroider a dot in the middle.

11 Once you have embroidered and filled in all the circles on both sides of the pillow, complete the decoration by embroidering dots at even intervals in the remaining space among the circles, with saffron-yellow rayon thread, using running stitch.

TEMPLATE / DESIGN AND COLOR PLAN

18in/45cm sq

12 Remove the fabric from the embroidery hoop by loosening the outer screw and gently easing it out (this helps to prevent marking the velvet). Press the velvet lightly on the wrong side with a dry iron using a fairly low heat.

ASSEMBLY

Cut out the front and the back pillow pieces. Place them right sides together with edges matching. On one edge, sew a 2in (5cm) long seam in from each end using red cotton thread, leaving an opening for the zipper. Insert the zipper

(see Basic Techniques page 133). Stitch around the other three sides. Trim the seams and clip the corners. Turn the cover right side out and ease out the corners with a pin; finger-press the edges. Steam-press the velvet. Insert the pillow form and close the zipper.

ZIGZAG BOLSTER

THE GRAPHIC SHAPES and simple yet bold color schemes used in old-fashioned children's games and toys provided the source of inspiration for this bolster. The strong but simple design works well on the cylindrical form. Wide zigzag shapes in bright colors are appliquéd onto a silk background. In the spaces between the zigzags, fine angular and vertical lines, and small dots are embroidered. The overall effect is striking and lively, adding a stylish accessory to any plain sofa.

Buttons

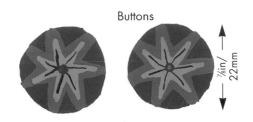

⅞in /
22mm

TEMPLATE / DESIGN AND COLOR PLAN

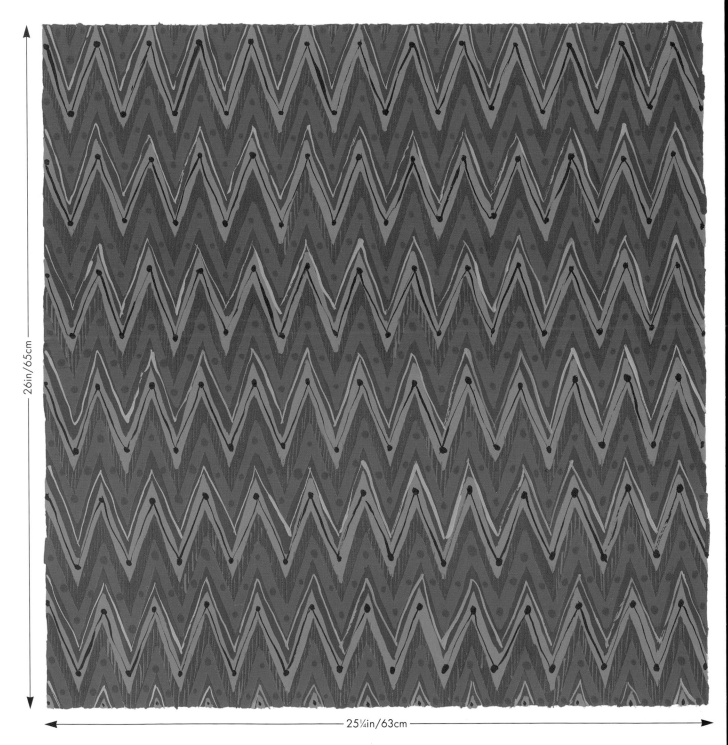

26in/65cm

25¼in/63cm

EQUIPMENT AND MATERIALS

Basic sewing kit (see page 124)

1¼yd (1m) terracotta silk dupion

16in (40cm) double-sided
    fusible webbing

28in (70cm) each of ocher and
    purple silk dupion

Golden-yellow, burgundy, deep-
    purple, shocking-pink, turquoise,
    and emerald-green rayon threads

Terracotta cotton sewing thread

14in (35cm) zipper

2 x ⅞in (22mm) self-cover buttons

Bolster pad 18in (45cm) long and
    6¼in (17cm) in diameter

◆ *Enlarge the bolster template by
362%. The button templates are shown
actual size.*

1 Lay the terracotta silk on a flat
surface. Measure in 4in (10cm)
from one side and the bottom edge.
Using tailor's chalk, mark the central
area with dots, then draw a 25¼ x 26in
(63 x 65cm) rectangle, within the dots.
Baste around the chalk line, which
includes a ⅜in (1.5cm) seam allowance.
Trace one of the button templates and
draw two buttons with tailor's chalk
onto the terracotta silk.

2 Enlarge the bolster template and
trace a single zigzag line. Calculate
the number of zigzags for both the
ocher and the purple silk. Draw the
zigzags and stars (buttons) on fusible
webbing, marking the color. Cut out
the shapes and fuse them to the
relevant–colored silk (see Basic
Techniques page 127). Cut out the
shapes. Fuse the ocher stars on top of
the purple stars. Remove the backing
paper and place the shapes on the silk,
following the design and color plan.
Space the zigzags 1in (2.5cm) apart.
Fuse in place.

3 Place the fabric in an embroidery
hoop, so that it is taut. Referring to
the plan, embroider as follows:

Golden yellow Embroider around
both edges of the ocher silk zigzags
with satin stitch, set at stitch width 3.

Burgundy Embroider a dot in the
middle of the point at one end of the
ocher silk zigzag, stitch a diagonal line
to the next point and embroider a dot,
using running stitch. Repeat this
along the whole length of each of the
ocher zigzags (see the diagram).

Deep purple Embroider around both

edges of the purple silk zigzags with
satin stitch, set at stitch width 3.

Shocking pink Embroider a dot in
every point, and half-way between
the points, of the purple silk zigzags.

Turquoise Stitch a single line of
running stitch down the middle,
following the zigzag, in the space
between the ocher and the purple
silk zigzags.

Emerald green Fill in the space
between the purple and ocher silk
zigzags with vertical lines stitched very
close together in running stitch (see
the diagram).

4 Embroider the buttons as follows:
Deep purple Embroider around
the purple silk star with satin stitch,

set at stitch width 2.5.

Golden yellow Embroider around the
ocher silk star with satin stitch, set at
stitch width 2.5.

Burgundy Starting in the middle of
the ocher star, stitch a line out to the
end of one point and back to the
middle again, then repeat for all the
remaining points.

5 Loosen the outer ring of the
embroidery hoop and carefully
remove the embroidered fabric. Press
with a warm iron.

ASSEMBLY

Cut out the bolster piece. Lay the long
edges together, right sides facing and
corners matching, and pin. Sew a 6in
(15cm) long seam in from each end
with terracotta cotton thread, leaving an
opening for the zipper. Insert the zipper
(see Basic Techniques page 133).

Turn in a ⅝in (1.5cm) hem at each
end, and stitch. Stitch a row of running
stitches along the hem, gather the ends,
and fasten securely to close the opening
(see the diagram).

Cover the two buttons with the
embroidered fabric (see instructions on
page 83) and attach them to the middle
of each end of the bolster (see the
diagram). Place the bolster pad inside
the cover and close the zipper.

FLORAL BOX CUSHION

THE INSPIRATION for this box cushion came from a beautiful wrought iron panel I spotted in the Victoria and Albert Museum in London. The panel had a large star flower as its focus, which was surrounded by entwined spiraling leaves and plants. The glorious color palette for this design is taken from the tones of nature, using a combination of silk, chiffon, and velvet. These are appliquéd onto a dense black velvet background, which allows the colors to radiate. Bold silk stripes around the sides of the box cushion contrast with, and set off, the flamboyant floral design.

EQUIPMENT AND MATERIALS

Basic sewing kit (see page 124)

1¾yd (1.5m) black velvet

1¼yd (1m) double-sided
  fusible webbing

16in (40cm) dark-green silk dupion

Small piece each of bottle-green,
  olive, leaf-green, dusty-pink,
  scarlet, and turquoise silk
  dupion

Small piece of bright-yellow
  velvet

Small piece each of deep-blue and
  deep-fuchsia silk chiffon

Dark-green, leaf-green, bottle-
  green, olive, dusty-pink,
  scarlet, turquoise, bright-
  yellow, deep-blue, deep-fuchsia,
  and gray rayon threads

Dark-green/white and leaf-green/
  white shaded rayon threads

Black cotton sewing thread

24in (60cm) zipper

4 x 22 x 22in (10 x 55 x 55cm) box
  cushion pad

◆ *Enlarge the template by 250%*

1 Enlarge the cushion templates to
the correct size. Lay the velvet on a
flat surface. Measure and mark on the
velvet two 22 x 22in (55 x 55cm)
squares, two 4 x 20in (10 x 50cm) sides,
one 4 x 22in (10 x 55cm) side, and two
2 x 26in (5 x 65cm) sides (the split side

KEY

DG Dark-green silk

LG Leaf-green silk

BG Bottle-green silk

O   Olive silk

Y   Bright-yellow velvet

DP Dusty-pink silk

S   Scarlet silk

T   Turquoise silk

B   Blue chiffon

F   Deep-fuchsia chiffon

TEMPLATES FOR CUSHION TOP AND SIDES

22in/55cm sq

25¼in/63cm

DG
DG
DG
DG
DG
DG
DG
DG
DG
DG
DG
DG
DG

piece) using tailor's chalk. Baste around the chalk line. Draw a ⅝in (1.5cm) seam allowance around all the pieces.

2 Trace the templates. Draw the shapes for the cushion front and the stripes for the sides on fusible webbing. Following the design and color plan, mark the colors with a pencil. Cut out the shapes roughly and fuse them to the relevant-colored silk, velvet or chiffon (see Basic Techniques page 127). Cut out the shapes. Remove the backing paper and place the shapes on the velvet. Then fuse the shapes in place using the tip of an iron at a fairly high temperature.

3 Insert the velvet in an embroidery hoop but do not make the hoop too tight as this will mark the fabric. Embroider the fabric as follows:
Dark green Embroider around the same-colored leaves with satin stitch, set at stitch width 3.
Leaf green Repeat as for dark green.
Bottle green Embroider around the same-colored leaves with satin stitch, set at stitch width 3. Fill in each leaf with concentric leaf shapes, using a single line of running stitch.
Olive Embroider as for bottle green.
Shaded dark green/white Stitch the stalk, central stalk, and main and minor veins onto the dark-green silk leaves in running stitch. Using satin stitch set first at stitch width 5, start at the top of the central stalk, and embroider a line tapering down to the tip of the leaf, ending in stitch width 0. Repeat on the four main veins.
Shaded leaf green/white Embroider as for dark green/white.
Dusty pink Embroider around the same-colored scroll and circle with satin stitch, set at stitch width 3. Stitch a line down the middle of each petal of the

bright-yellow velvet flower in satin stitch, set at stitch width 2.
Scarlet Embroider around the same-colored scroll with satin stitch, set at stitch width 3.
Turquoise Embroider as for scarlet.
Bright yellow Embroider around the same-colored flower with satin stitch, set at stitch width 3.
Deep blue Embroider around the same-colored long flower and wings with satin stitch, set at stitch width 3. Fill in each long flower with two lines of running stitch up the stalk, the leaves with concentric leaf shapes, and the flower head with concentric flower head shapes, using one line of stitching (see the diagram). Fill in the wings with

concentric wing shapes, using one line of stitching. Stitch a zigzag line on the dusty-pink circle. Fill in the middle of the flower with dots, linked in a spiral.
Deep fuchsia Embroider around and through the middle of the same-colored leaf, using satin stitch set at stitch width 3. Stitch two lines of running stitch down both sides of the leaf, following the shape.

4 Embroider the sides as follows:
Gray Embroider around the dark-green silk stripes using satin stitch, set at stitch width 3.

Dark green On every alternate dark-green silk stripe, embroider four vertical lines of running stitch.

5 Carefully remove the fabric from the hoop, which helps to prevent marking the velvet. Press the velvet lightly on the wrong side using a dry iron at a low heat.

ASSEMBLY
Cut out all the pieces. Lay the two pieces of the split back strip together, with right sides facing, and pin. Sew a 1in (2.5cm) long seam in from each end with black cotton thread, leaving an opening for the zipper. Insert the zipper (see Basic Techniques page 133).

Stitch the ends of the side pieces together to form a circle by joining the two shorter strips to each end of the front strip (long), and joining the back strip between the two shorter strips (see the diagram). Check that the resulting ring fits closely around the cushion pad.

Pin the edges of the top piece to the edges of the sides, right sides together. Stitch around all the edges. Repeat for the bottom piece. Trim the seams and clip the corners. Turn the cover right side out and finger-press the edges. Steam-press the velvet. Put the pad inside the cover and close the zipper.

DESIGN AND COLOR PLAN FOR CUSHION TOP

DESIGN AND COLOR PLAN FOR SIDES

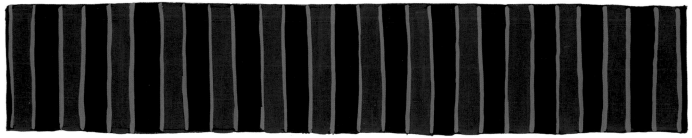

BLUEBELLS TIEBACK

A DECORATIVE wrought-iron balustrade panel inspired this piece of embroidery. The design reminded me of the paper cutouts of people and shapes that I had made as a child. For the base fabric of the tieback, I used a dark-blue cotton satin. The main shape, which is repeated continuously along the length of the piece, is a light-colored silk. Two colors are used for the delicate, embroidered bluebells and they are placed alternately on top of the light-colored silk of the main shape.

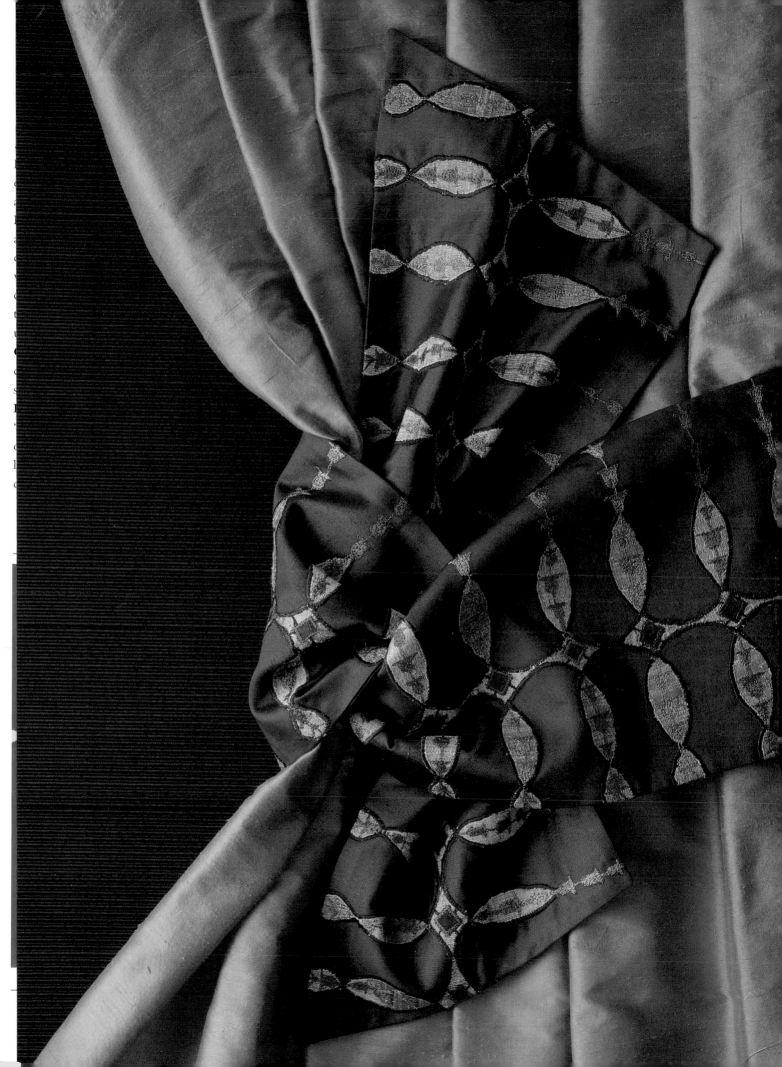

SCROLLS TIEBACK

ORNATE WROUGHT-IRONWORK was the starting point for this embroidered curtain tieback. To retain the fluidity of the design, a flower section is placed side by side with a reversed flower section, and the two are joined together with an overlapping tendril. Extra flowers and tendrils are added, reaching out to the sides. The rounded edges of the tieback echo the curved nature of the design. To create a truly elaborate Victorian feel, the shapes are all embroidered in colored silks which are then applied to a rich, velvet background.

TEMPLATE / DESIGN AND COLOR PLAN

30⅜in/76cm

EQUIPMENT AND MATERIALS

Basic sewing kit (see page 124)

1¼yd (1m) burgundy velvet

16in (40cm) double-sided
    fusible webbing

16in (40cm) each of silvery–green
    and dusty-pink silk dupion

Small pieces each of terracotta,
    deep-blue, and mauve silk
    dupion

Silvery-green, sienna, dusty-
    pink, terracotta, deep-blue,
    and mauve rayon threads

20in (50cm) heavyweight
    iron-on interfacing

4½yd (4m) piping cord

Burgundy cotton sewing thread

4 curtain rings

2 hooks

◆ *Enlarge the template by 224%. To*
enlarge the template to fit your own
tieback measurements, multiply your
length measurement by 100 and then
divide that figure by 13½in/34cm to
get the percentage enlargement.

1 Enlarge the tieback template as instructed. (If you like, you can figure out the exact length you want your tieback to be by draping a tape measure loosely around your curtain and holding the ends where the finished tieback will hook to the wall. Then decide how wide you want the tieback to be. Enlarge the template as instructed, using the calculation.) You will need a piece of fabric that is twice these dimensions for each tieback, and piping cord to go around both tiebacks. Your template will measure 16.5 x 76cm (6½ x 30⅜in), or your chosen dimensions.

Lay the velvet down on a flat surface, pin the template to the velvet, and draw around the edge neatly with tailor's chalk. Baste around the chalked line, then draw a ⅝in (1.5cm) seam allowance around the entire piece. Using the template, draw out a further three pieces (you will be embroidering two of these, one for each tieback). Baste around the chalk line and draw a seam allowance around each.

2 Trace the template. Referring to the design and color plan, figure out the colors and fabric to be used for each shape. Draw all the shapes on fusible webbing, marking the color with a pencil. Cut out the shapes roughly and fuse them to the relevant–colored silk (see Basic Techniques page 127). Cut out the shapes, remove the backing paper and place the shapes on the velvet, following the plan. Once you are satisfied with the arrangement of the shapes, fuse them in position using the tip of the iron at a fairly high temperature and pressing gently around each shape. Be careful not to mark or flatten the pile of the velvet as you are doing this.

3 Untighten the screw of an embroidery hoop to make it quite loose and place it around the velvet. Then tighten the hoop again, being careful not to make it too tight, as this will mark the fabric. Referring to the design and color plan, embroider the fabric as follows:

6½in/16.5cm

Silvery green Embroider around the same-colored silk scrolls with satin stitch, set at stitch width 2.5. Where indicated in the template, embroider long corkscrews or spirals, using four rows of running stitch (see the diagram).

Sienna Embroider a line running through the center of the silk scrolls, following the shape, with a single line of running stitch.

Dusty pink Embroider around the same-colored flowers with satin stitch, set at stitch width 2.5.

Terracotta Embroider around the same-colored flowers with satin stitch, set at stitch width 2.5.

Deep blue Embroider around the same-colored circles with satin stitch, set at stitch width 2.5. Using running stitch, embroider two lines halfway up each petal on the terracotta silk flower, returning to the center each time.

Mauve Embroider around the same-colored circles with satin stitch, set at stitch width 2.5. Embroider the lines on each petal as with the deep-blue thread.

4 Remove the fabric from the embroidery hoop by loosening the screw and gently easing it out (to prevent marking the velvet). Carefully press the velvet lightly on the wrong side using a dry iron set on low heat.

ASSEMBLY

Cut out the two front and two back pieces, then the two pieces from interfacing fabric. Fuse them to the wrong side of the back pieces. Make the piping in dusty-pink

silk dupion (see Basic Techniques pages 133). Lay the piping on the right side of the embroidered piece, with the raw edges matching and the piping's stitching line along the tieback's seamline. Pin the piping in place, snipping into the seam allowance of the piping around the curves. Using a zipper foot, sew along the piping's stitching line, with burgundy cotton thread. To join the corded piping together, overlap the ends by 2in (5cm), unpick the stitches of the covered cord, and trim the cord so that the ends meet. Then fold the fabric back over the piping cord, turn in a small hem, and slipstitch in place.

Lay the plain piece of burgundy velvet on top of the embroidered piece, with right sides together and raw edges matching. Pin and sew through all layers just inside the previous row of stitching, leaving a 4¾in (12cm) opening along one edge. Turn the tieback right side out. Slipstitch the opening to close. Sew a curtain ring to each end. Mount the wall-hooks.

117

CHRISTMAS DECORATIONS

THESE DECORATIONS EXPLORE different shapes and forms. The two-sided square uses circles, squares, rays, and chevrons. Intensely colored velvets are used for the circular shapes, which are applied to richly shaded silk backgrounds. Each facet of the three-sided diamond is decorated differently. The facets themselves are halved and quartered, and each section is given its own design of squares, waves, zigzags, diamonds, stars, stripes, dots, fleurs-de-lis, and corals. Strongly colored velvets, silks and threads are applied against richly toned silk backgrounds. Metallic thread is used to add a wonderfully festive feeling to the decoration. The two-sided star exploits the basic shape, placing stars of different colors and sizes within other stars. The colors are bold and vibrant – in silk, satin, and velvet on a golden-yellow silk base.

TWO-SIDED SQUARE

EQUIPMENT AND MATERIALS

Basic sewing kit (see page 124)

10 x 10in (25 x 25cm) golden-yellow and deep-blue silk dupion

4in (10cm) double-sided fusible webbing

Small piece each of dark-purple and red velvet

Dark-purple, dark-orange, turquoise, red, bright-orange, bright-pink, and saffron-yellow rayon threads

Cotton sewing thread

Strong turquoise thread

Potpourri or polyester stuffing

◆ *Enlarge the template by 200%*

1 Lay the golden-yellow and deep-blue silk dupion on a flat surface. Measure and draw a 4 x 4in (10 x 10cm) square on both pieces with tailor's chalk. Baste around the chalk line. Draw a ⅜in (1.5cm) seam allowance around both pieces.

2 Enlarge and trace the template. Following the design and color plan, figure out the color to be used for each circle. Draw all the circles on fusible webbing, marking the color. Cut out the circles roughly and fuse them to the relevant-colored velvet (see Basic Techniques page 127). Cut out the circles. Remove the backing paper and place the circles on the silk squares. Fuse in position.

3 Place the fabric in an embroidery hoop. Following the design and color plan, embroider the golden yellow square as follows:
Dark purple Embroider around the same-colored velvet circles with satin stitch, set at stitch width 3.
Dark orange Embroider a spiral on the small dark-purple velvet circle, from

TEMPLATES / DESIGN AND COLOR PLAN

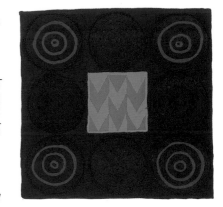

4in/10cm sq

the center out to the sides, with a single line of running stitch. Stitch around the small velvet circle, then embroider 28 lines radiating out to the large velvet circle. Fill in alternate sections with densely packed vertical lines of stitching (see the diagram).
Turquoise Embroider four evenly spaced circles onto the large dark-purple velvet circle, with a single line of running stitch. Stitch around the large velvet circle, then embroider 64 lines radiating out to the edges of the square. Fill in alternate sections with densely packed vertical lines of stitching.

4 Following the design and color plan, embroider the deep-blue square as follows:
Red Embroider around all the same colored velvet circles with satin

stitch, set at stitch width 3.
Bright orange Embroider three concentric circles on the four red velvet circles at each corner of the square, with three lines of running stitch.
Bright pink: Embroider as with the bright-orange thread on the remaining red velvet circles.
Saffron yellow Using running stitch, stitch the outline of a 1⅜ x 1⅜in (3.5 x 3.5cm) square in the middle. Divide this into three columns, and draw in chevron shapes. Fill in every alternate chevron with densely packed vertical lines of stitching.
Turquoise Fill in the remaining chevrons with densely packed vertical lines of running stitch.

5 Remove the fabric from the embroidery hoop and press.

ASSEMBLY

Cut out the two square pieces. Lay the pieces together, with right sides facing and edges matching. Pin and stitch all around with the cotton sewing thread, leaving a 1½in (4cm) opening along one edge. Trim, and clip the corners, then turn right side out. Using the strong turquoise thread, stitch through one corner, make a loop, and secure in place. Fill with potpourri or polyester stuffing. Slipstitch the opening securely.

TWO-SIDED STAR

EQUIPMENT AND MATERIALS

Basic sewing kit (see page 124)
6 x 6in (15 x 15cm) cardboard
8in (20cm) double-sided fusible webbing
Small piece each of golden-yellow, turquoise, and red silk dupion
Small piece of dark-purple velvet
Red, turquoise, and dark-purple rayon threads
Gold metallic thread
Cotton sewing thread
Polyester stuffing
Strong turquoise thread

◆ *Enlarge the template by 200%*

1 Enlarge one of the star templates and make a cardboard template. Lay the golden-yellow silk dupion on a flat surface. Draw two stars on the silk dupion with tailor's chalk. Baste around the chalk line. Draw a ⅝in (1.5cm) seam allowance around both pieces.

2 Trace the enlarged template. Following the design and color plan, work out the color and fabric to be used for each star. Draw all the stars on fusible webbing, marking the colors. Cut out the stars roughly and fuse them to the relevant silk or velvet (see Basic Techniques page 127). Cut out the stars. Remove the backing paper and place the cutout stars on the silk stars. Fuse in position.

3 Place the fabric in an embroidery hoop, and embroider as follows:
Red Embroider around the edges of the same-colored silk stars with satin stitch, at stitch width 2.5. Stitch around the outer edges of the central red silk star with satin stitch, at stitch width 2.5. Stitch a single zigzag line from the outer edge to the edge of the deep-purple velvet star, stitching right around the star, in running stitch. Stitch a star in the middle of the turquoise silk star, with densely packed running stitch.
Turquoise Embroider around the edges of the same-colored silk stars with satin stitch, at stitch width 2.5. Stitch around the outer edges of the central turquoise silk star with satin stitch, at stitch width 2.5. Stitch a single zigzag line from the outer edge to the edge of the red star, stitching right around the star, in running stitch.
Dark purple Embroider around the edges of the same-colored velvet star with satin stitch, set at stitch width 2.5. Stitch a star in the middle of the red silk star, in densely packed running stitch.
Metallic gold Following the shape, stitch a single line inside each star.

4 Remove the fabric from the embroidery hoop and press.

ASSEMBLY

Cut out the two star pieces. Pin them together, with right sides facing. Stitch around the edges with the cotton sewing thread, leaving the top point open. Trim, and clip the corners, then turn right side out. Fill with polyester stuffing up to where the stitching ends. Gradually slipstitch the sides of the point as you stuff it. Stitch through one corner with strong turquoise thread, make a loop, and secure in place.

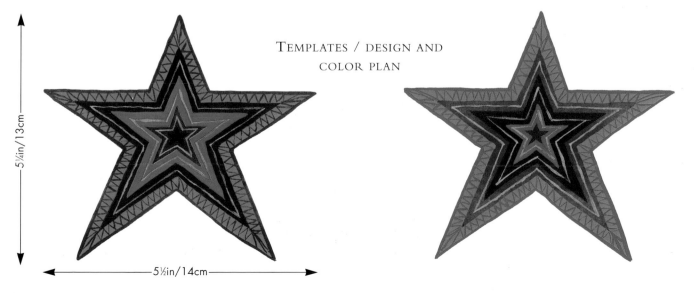

TEMPLATES / DESIGN AND
COLOR PLAN

5¼in/13cm

5½in/14cm

THREE-SIDED DIAMOND

EQUIPMENT AND MATERIALS
Basic sewing kit (see page 124)
6⅜ x 4in (16 x 10cm) cardboard
10 x 10in (25 x 25cm) mauve, deep
  cerise, and terracotta silk dupion
8in (20cm) double-sided fusible webbing
Scraps of ice-blue, purple, bright-
  yellow, red, deep-turquoise, and
  saffron-yellow silk dupion
Scraps of dark-purple, deep-red,
  deep-blue, orange, and sage velvet
Dark-purple, leaf-green, saffron-yellow,
  pale-turquoise, bright-orange,
  deep-turquoise, ice-blue, yellow,
  and sage-green rayon threads
Gold metallic thread
Cotton sewing thread
Strong turquoise thread
Polyester stuffing
Small red beads
Strong red thread

◆ *Enlarge the template by 203%*

1 Enlarge one of the diamond
  templates to the correct size and
make a cardboard template. Lay the
pieces of mauve, deep-cerise and
terracotta silk dupion on a flat surface.
Draw a diamond on each of the pieces,
using tailor's chalk. Baste around the
chalk line. Draw a ⅝in (1.5cm) seam
allowance around each piece.

2 Trace each of the templates.
  Following the templates and the
design and color plan, figure out the
color and fabric to be used for each
shape. Draw out all the shapes on
fusible webbing, marking the color
of each shape in pencil. Cut the shapes
out roughly and fuse them to the
relevant-colored silk or velvet (see Basic
Techniques page 127). Cut out the
shapes, then remove the backing paper

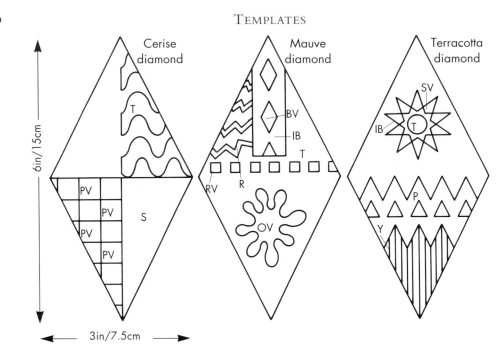

6in/15cm

3in/7.5cm

Cerise diamond

Mauve diamond

Terracotta diamond

and place the shapes on the diamonds,
following the templates and plan. Once
you are pleased with the arrangement,
fuse the shapes in position.

3 Place the fabric in an embroidery
  hoop. Following the design and
color plan, embroider the deep-cerise
diamond as follows:
Dark purple Embroider around the
edges of the same-colored squares with
satin stitch, set at stitch width 2 (to
achieve a checkerboard pattern).
Leaf green Embroider around the
edges of the deep-turquoise silk waves
with satin stitch, set at stitch width 2.
Fill in the spaces between the waves
with evenly spaced vertical lines of
running stitch. Embroider a cross in
the cerise squares of the checkerboard,
using two rows of running stitch.
Saffron yellow Embroider around the
edges of the same-colored silk triangle
with satin stitch, set at stitch width 2.
Embroider dots along the deep
turquoise silk waves, in running stitch.
Pale turquoise Stitch seven vertical
lines down the saffron-yellow silk

KEY
T   Deep-turquoise silk
PV   Dark-purple velvet
S   Saffron-yellow silk
R   Red silk
IB   Ice-blue silk
BV   Deep-blue velvet
RV   Deep-red velvet
OV   Orange velvet
SV   Sage-green velvet
P   Purple silk
Y   Bright-yellow silk

DESIGN AND COLOR PLAN

triangle, using two rows of running stitch, then slash down the lines with sharp scissors. In the remaining segment of the cerise diamond, embroider four fleurs-de-lis using densely packed running stitch (see the diagram). Stitch five crosses in the remaining spaces, using running stitch.

4 Following the plan, embroider the mauve diamond as follows:
Bright orange Embroider around the edges of the same-colored velvet coral shape and the red silk zigzags with satin stitch, set at stitch width 2.
Deep turquoise Embroider around the edges of the same colored silk triangle with satin stitch, set at stitch width 2. Embroider a circle in the middle of the orange velvet coral in running stitch, and fill in with a densely packed spiral. Embroider evenly spaced dots around the coral in the bottom half of the diamond, using running stitch.
Leaf green Embroider around the edges of the deep-red velvet boxes with satin stitch, set at stitch width 2. Stitch a zigzag line in the space above the velvet

boxes, using a running stitch.
Ice blue Embroider around the edges of the same-colored silk strip with satin stitch, set at stitch width 2.
Saffron yellow Embroider four rows of connected dots along the length of the deep-turquoise silk triangle, using running stitch.
Metallic gold Embroider around the edges of the deep-blue velvet diamonds with satin stitch, set at stitch width 2.

5 Following the plan, embroider the terracotta diamond as follows:
Yellow Fill in the top half of the diamond with horizontal lines of running stitch.
Dark purple Embroider evenly-spaced dots on top of the yellow horizontal lines, using running stitch. Embroider around the edges of the yellow-silk stripes with satin stitch, set at stitch width 2.
Pale turquoise Embroider around the edges of the same-colored silk star points and the cut-out triangles on the purple silk zigzag strip with satin stitch, set at stitch width 2.

Sage green Embroider around the edges of the same-colored velvet star with satin stitch, set at stitch width 2.
Deep turquoise Embroider around the edges of the same-colored circle with satin stitch, set at stitch width 2. Embroider small stars with densely packed running stitch, in between the points of the purple silk zigzag.
Metallic gold Embroider around the edges of the dark-purple silk zigzag strip with satin stitch, set at stitch width 2. Stitch two zigzag lines above and below the cut-out triangles using running stitch. Embroider a star in the center of the deep-turquoise circle with densely packed running stitches.

6 Gently ease the fabric out of the hoop and then press the fabric on the wrong side with a warm iron.

ASSEMBLY
Cut out the three diamond pieces. Place the mauve and the deep-cerise pieces together, right sides facing and edges matching. Pin and stitch up one side with the cotton thread. Trim, and clip the corners. Place the terracotta and the deep-cerise pieces together, right sides facing and edges matching. Pin and stitch up one side. Trim, and clip the corners. Pin the terracotta piece to the mauve piece and stitch halfway up one side, including a corner. Check that all the points of the diamonds meet.

Turn right side out, and ease out the corners using a pin. Using the strong turquoise thread, stitch through the top point, make a loop, and secure in place. Fill the diamond with polyester stuffing. Slipstitch the opening securely. Using a strong red thread, string ten beads, and stitch them securely into the bottom point. Repeat so that you finish with two loops of red beads hanging from the diamond.

EQUIPMENT AND MATERIALS

GENERAL EQUIPMENT

Sewing machine There are many sewing machines on the market that are designed for creating embroidery. They range from basic models with a few automatic patterns and the ability to embroider freestyle, to sophisticated computerized machines with memory cards and a huge bank of automatic patterns. Some sewing machines can be linked to computers. To use them, you first design an elaborate pattern, then load it into the machine, and the design is embroidered automatically onto your fabric. Although you do not need a state-of-the-art sewing machine to undertake the projects in this book, the one feature you must have on your machine is the ability to embroider freestyle, which allows you to draw onto your fabric with the machine.

To do machine embroidery, you need an electric sewing machine with a "feed dog" that can be lowered by a lever or covered with a cover plate. This allows you to sew in all directions – forward, backward, sideways, and diagonally. A removable bobbin case is essential, so that you can adjust the tension when you use thick embroidery threads. For free embroidery, you will need a darning or freestyle embroidery foot which has a spring mechanism that moves up and down with the needle, allowing you to stitch in any direction. Most machines have a darning foot but, if not, you can remove the foot completely. Be careful that your fingers do not get caught. It is advisable to keep your machine well maintained by brushing out the bobbin case after each use, and oiling the machine regularly. **Iron** A dry iron is best for fusing webbing to fabric. (It is advisable to

keep one especially for this purpose.) A steam iron is needed to press the fabrics and the finished garments. **Velvet board** A stainless steel bristled board for pressing velvet – the bristles prevent the pile from being flattened.

BASIC SEWING KIT

Embroidery hoop or frame It is essential to use a hoop or frame for free machine embroidery to keep the fabric taut. An adjustable, round wooden frame is ideal. Before you start, bind the inner ring with strips of cotton cut on the bias or seam tape, to help grip the fabric and protect your embroidery. **Scissors** You will need three pairs to make the projects in this book: paper scissors for cutting out patterns, fusible webbing, and batting; sharp embroidery scissors for cutting and slashing; and dressmaking scissors for fabrics. **Needles** Keep a selection of machine needles in various sizes. As a rule, the thicker the thread and fabric you are using, the larger the needle required. Also useful is a selection of sharps or betweens needles for hand sewing, and No. 10 quilting needles for quilting. **Dressmaker's steel pins** Long thin pins are used for most work. Large glass-headed pins are good for assembling quilts and thick fabrics. **Basting thread** Any type of cotton thread is suitable for basting. **Tape measure** A non-stretch tape measure in both inches and centimeters is best. For quilting and large projects, you can obtain a tape measure that is twice as long as a normal one. **Ruler** A ruler is useful for checking measurements in a pattern. **Tissue, tracing, or layout paper** These are used for tracing designs.

Transfer the design onto fabric by stitching around the design, then tearing the paper away. **Dressmaking pattern paper** Use this for tracing or making patterns, and to scale-up a design. **Masking tape** This tape can be lifted off of paper or fabric without tearing or marking it. Use it to keep fabric and paper in position when tracing designs. **Tailor's chalk** Use this for transferring patterns to fabric. It can be rubbed off of fabric easily without leaving a mark. **Pencils** Sharp pencils are essential for tracing designs on fusible webbing and dissolvable fabrics. **Marking pens** The ink from water/air-erasable pens disappears in water and within two weeks in air. Transfer pencils can be ironed onto the fabric.

MATERIALS

Silks Natural fabrics are the best for embroidery, and I prefer using silks in their many forms:

Dupion has a natural slub effect and is ideal for vests.

Crêpe satin is a high-sheen fabric with a lovely weight that is good for lining vests.

Crêpe de Chine is a lightweight fabric with lovely drape, that is perfect for scarves and shirts.

Crêpe georgette is a heavy, more transparent fabric, that is perfect for scarves and shirts.

Crêpe mousseline and chiffon are sheer transparent fabrics, flowing beautifully as scarves and shirts.

Habotai silk is a lightweight fabric that is ideal for lining. **Velvets** Velvets are wonderful for their richness. I use the following types:

Silk velvet has a beautiful luster

and feel – ideal for scarves and vests.

Cotton velvet is hard-wearing and has a matte quality that is perfect for home furnishings.

Plain and shot viscose velvet have a wonderful rich sheen that is ideal for vests, scarves, and furnishings.

Cotton satin This has a pronounced sheen on one side, is hard-wearing, and a practical choice for home furnishings.

Interfacing Iron-on interfacing is available in various weights, adding body and stiffening fabrics.

Double-sided fusible webbing This comes on a transfer paper backing; when the webbing is ironed, it fuses fabric together.

Dissolvable fabrics These allow you to produce machine-made lace. The lace is stitched to the fabric as a means of support, and the fabric is then dissolved, leaving the stitching intact.

Hot-water dissolvable fabric is a turquoise woven fabric which disappears when immersed in boiling water. The cold-water variety is a clear plastic fabric that disappears when it is immersed in cold water.

Vanishing muslin is a firm, woven fabric that can be burned away in contact with a hot iron.

THREADS

Various threads are used for the projects in this book.

Rayon threads These are strong threads of a high quality, with a wonderful silky luster and available in a huge choice of colours. They come in two weights: No. 40 is a lovely, fine thread which I tend to use most; No. 30 is thicker and more lustrous, and is good for definite lines.

Metallic threads These range from glittery metallic and lurex to textured threads. They are high quality and available in a choice of colors, in various weights.

Cotton threads Mercerized cottons are suitable for hand and machine embroidery. Stranded, pearl, and *coton à broder* are hand embroidery threads that are available in a large selection of colors; they can be used in the bobbin for machine embroidery.

Chenille Normally used for knitting, chenille can be successful in machine embroidery if used in the bobbin. It gives a lovely textured effect.

Wool yarns Tapestry and crewel wool are hand embroidery threads, but both can be used in the bobbin for machine embroidery.

Shirring elastic Used in the bobbin, this can produce wonderful three-dimensional texture.

BASIC TECHNIQUES

USING A HOOP OR FRAME

It is essential to use a hoop for all types of machine embroidery to keep the fabric taut. The hoop is used in reverse for hand embroidery. Lay the outer ring down, place the fabric on top, right side facing, then insert the inner ring. Tighten the screw, easing the fabric flat until it is as taut as a drum.

The frame is inserted under the needle on a sewing machine and sits on the machine bed. Hold the frame at both sides and then move it in all directions as you stitch.

HOW TO MACHINE EMBROIDER

Machine embroidery can be done with a presser foot, but a freestyle embroidery foot gives you greater freedom of movement. For both methods, experiment on spare fabric to learn how to control the machine, and how to manipulate your fabrics.

The thread that is being used will determine the size of the needle. There is a groove running down the length of the needle, and the thread should lie in this. If you use too fine a needle, the thread will not fit into the groove and this will give you skipped stitches. I find

that a No. 90 is suitable as it is strong enough to withstand the strain and speed of this type of work.

The bobbin spool case should be removable, and needs to have a small metal piece at the side which is attached by a small screw. This can be loosened to alter the tension – but do this very carefully with small adjustments; you can lose the screw very easily.

USING THE PRESSER FOOT

Set up the machine as usual and experiment with the straight stitch and the zigzag stitch. By varying the tension and using different threads on top and in the spool, you should achieve interesting textural and color effects.

Vary the stitch length and width, and experiment changing from straight stitch to satin stitch. A variety of patterns and decorative devices can be created this way, providing a good introduction to machine embroidery.

USING THE TAILOR-TACK FOOT

Set up the machine for zigzag stitch, attach the tailor-tack foot, and lower the presser foot. Set the stitch width from 2 up to 5 and loosen the top

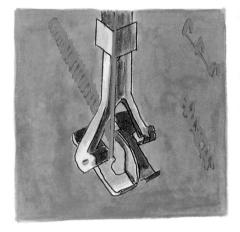

thread tension. Vary the stitch length and width to create a variety of textural and decorative effects. The smaller the stitch length, the denser the row of looped stitching. Spacing the stitching in intervals will give you a lighter general effect. Using two different-colored rayon threads on the top gives a thick, lustrous quality. If you are worried that your stitches will come out, try ironing a piece of lightweight interfacing to the back of the area that has been stitched.

USING THE FREESTYLE EMBROIDERY FOOT

For free embroidery, you will need a darning or freestyle embroidery foot, with the presser foot lever lowered to engage the top tension. Lower the feed dog and set the stitch width to zero. Place the frame under the needle, and lower the presser foot lever. Hold the thread taut with your left hand and insert the needle into the fabric to bring up the bobbin thread. Hold both threads tightly for the first few stitches, then cut them off. As the feed dog is lowered, the speed at which you move the fabric will determine the length of the stitch. Moving the hoop slowly with the needle moving fast will give a very small, tight stitch. Alternatively, moving the hoop fast will give you a long and very loose stitch.

Running stitch
Begin by moving the fabric slowly and start stitching. Move the fabric in all directions, and practice doodling and creating shapes and textures.

Zigzag stitch
By adjusting the stitch width, you will obtain a zigzag stitch that can be wide or narrow. Move the hoop slowly to achieve a close, dense satin stitch (this can be perfected with practice. If you move it fast, you will achieve a very open zigzag line.

Whip stitch
Use a cotton machine embroidery thread on the top and a rayon thread in

the bobbin, perhaps in a different color. By tightening the top tension and loosening the bobbin tension, you will create a loop of the bobbin thread – the bobbin thread whips around the top thread. This can be achieved using running or zigzag stitch. Decorative effects can be created by varying the tensions, movement, and speed.

Cable stitch
Use a thick embroidery cotton in the bobbin and a rayon thread on the top. Wind the thread evenly onto the bobbin, being careful not to overfill it, then place it in the bobbin case and loosen the tension screw until the thread can pass through the gap. Tighten the top tension and place the fabric in the embroidery hoop, wrong side up. This will give you a lovely couched or corded effect. Alter the tensions and experiment with different threads and yarns to obtain various interesting textural effects.

USING SHIRRING ELASTIC
Wind the shirring elastic onto the bobbin, holding it taut as you wind (if you wind it on too loose you will not get enough elasticity to distort the fabric). Place the bobbin in the case and loosen the tension screw until the thread can pass through the gap. Tighten the top tension, place the fabric in the embroidery hoop right side up, insert the needle into the fabric, and bring up the bobbin thread. Using running stitch, experiment with different patterns, grids, or connected circles and spirals, allowing space in between the stitching for the fabric to pucker. When you have finished, remove the fabric from the hoop and it will distort into interesting patterns. Keep practicing with different patterns and density of stitch until you are pleased with the results.

HOW TO APPLIQUÉ
Appliqué is the application of pieces of fabric to a flat ground. Wonderful spontaneous designs can be created using appliqué, which can be quilted and decorated with stitches. It is a popular method used to decorate garments, furnishings, and quilts.

Machine appliqué using fusible webbing
This is the method I prefer as it is quicker and especially good for fabrics that have a tendency to fray. Draw your shape on the paper side of the fusible

webbing, iron it to your chosen fabric, fusible side down, and cut it out. Remove the backing paper, place the shape on the background fabric, fusible side down, and press with an iron to bond them together.

Place the fabric in an embroidery hoop, making sure that it is taut. Using the freestyle embroidery foot, stitch around the shape using either running or satin stitch.

Remember that using fusible webbing will cause some of the shapes to come out as a mirror image of your design. To avoid this, draw the design on paper in reverse, then trace this on the fusible webbing.

Fusible webbing adds stiffness to the fabric, making it unsuitable for use in such projects as scarves, shirts, and curtains. These all need to retain fluidity of movement in the fabric to help with the drape.

Machine appliqué

Draw each shape on the fabric. Cut them out, adding ¼in (6mm) for a seam

allowance. Clip the curved edges close to the marked line, turn the seam allowance to the back, and baste down. Arrange and pin the appliquéd shapes onto the background fabric. Using the freestyle embroidery foot, stitch around the shapes with either running, zigzag, or satin stitch.

Hand appliqué

Draw each shape on the fabric and cut them out, adding ¼in (6mm) for a seam allowance. Clip the curved edges close to the marked line, turn the seam allowance to the back, and baste it down. Arrange, pin, and baste the

appliquéd shapes onto the background fabric. Slipstitch around the shape with matching thread, using small stitches.

USING DISSOLVABLE FABRIC

There are three types of dissolvable fabric: hot-water or cold-water dissolvable fabric and vanishing muslin.

Hot-water dissolvable fabric

This is a turquoise woven fabric which I prefer to use as it is strong and can withstand a large number of stitches without ripping. It is more expensive than the other types, but it is worth acquiring, especially for the Flowers Shirt project (see page 16). You can trace a design on the dissolvable fabric with a pencil, or design as you go

along. Place the fabric in a hoop, making sure it is taut. Use the same-color rayon thread in the bobbin and on the top. The principles are slightly different from normal free embroidery,

as the stitching must be self-supporting. Using running stitch, cover the area densely – but not too much, since this makes it very hard. Stitch horizontally, then vertically to bind the stitches together, so when you dissolve the fabric, they do not fall apart.

When you have finished your design, check the stitches to make sure that they are all connected. Remove the embroidery hoop and immerse the fabric in a pan of boiling water. Do not be alarmed when the piece distorts, as this is just the fabric melting. Boil the embroidery for 3 to 5 minutes, then

remove it and rinse it in cold water. If it feels hard, return it to the pan and boil for a few more minutes. When the embroidery feels soft and pliable, it is ready. Leave it to dry flat. When dry, press it with a steam iron.

You may need to practice this technique until you can manage to stitch a piece that does not fall apart.

Cold-water dissolvable fabric

This is a clear plastic fabric that can be used in the same way as the hot-water dissolvable fabric; the only difference is that this fabric is dissolved in cold water. If it feels hard after being immersed in cold water, repeat the process until it is soft and pliable.

Vanishing muslin

This is a firm, woven fabric that can be used in the same way as the hot-water dissolvable fabric. To remove the fabric after stitching, burn it away with a hot iron, then rub the piece between your fingers until all the fibers are removed.

TRANSFERRING DESIGNS

There are several ways of transferring your designs onto fabric. Choose the one that is the most suitable for your fabric or the intricacy of the design.

Chalk lines

Simple designs and shapes, or a design needing guidelines, can be drawn on fabric or marked with tailor's chalk or dressmaker's pencil. Check first that the marks can be rubbed off. This method is unsuitable for elaborate designs as the marks will wear off as you work.

Dressmaker's carbon paper

This comes in different colors that show up on either dark or light fabrics. Place the carbon paper face down on the fabric and lay the design on top. Trace the design using a dressmaker's tracing wheel or a sharp pencil.

Tracing through transparent fabric

Designs can be traced or drawn directly on transparent or lightweight thin fabrics. Place the design on a flat surface and secure in place with masking tape. Lay the fabric on top, smooth in place, and secure the edges with masking tape. Trace the design with a pencil or a water/air-erasable pen.

Tracing and stitching

This method is good for dark-colored and heavy fabrics. Trace the design on tissue or layout paper and pin it to the fabric. Stitch around the design, using the freestyle embroidery foot and a thread either the color of the fabric or one of the colors in your design. Carefully tear away the paper, leaving the stitched design. This line will be integral with the stitched design.

ENLARGING, REDUCING, AND REVERSING DESIGNS

Photocopying

This is the quickest and easiest method of reproducing. Some photocopiers can reduce or enlarge designs to your required size. Once you have become confident, you will find the machine an invaluable design tool.

Light box or window tracing

This method allows you to put your designs on paper in reverse, something you might need to do when using fusible webbing or a transfer pencil.

Anchor the design on the light box or window with masking tape, and trace the design with a pen or pencil.

SEWING STITCHES

Running stitch

This stitch can be used to secure fabrics in place, as decoration, or to make gathers. Work small, evenly spaced stitches, passing the needle over and under the fabric.

Stab stitch

This is running stitch made in a stabbing vertical movement. Pass the needle down through the fabric in one

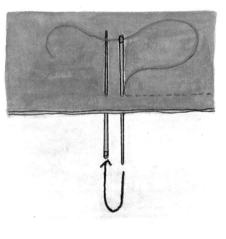

movement and up in the second, working small, evenly spaced stitches.

Slipstitch

This stitch is used to secure hems and edges invisibly. Slip the needle through

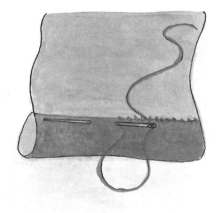

the folded edge, then pick up a thread of the main fabric close to the folded edge and pull through. Repeat, making small neat stitches along the length.

Basting

This stitch is a temporary one to hold fabric in position. Make long and short running stitches along the fabric.

SEAMS

Flat fell seam

Pin the right sides together and sew a

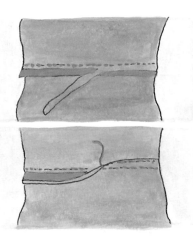

seam. Trim the back seam allowance (only) to ¼ in (6mm). Press the front seam allowance over the trimmed edge (back seam). Turn in ¼in (6mm) on the remaining allowance, press, and stitch.

French seam

Pin the wrong sides together and sew a seam ¼in (6mm) in from the edge. Press

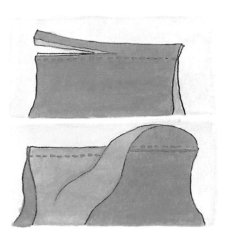

the seam open and trim. With right sides together, fold the fabric along the seam, then sew another seam ½in (12mm) in from the edge, to enclose the raw edges. Press.

Understitch

Open out the facing of the garment and stitch it to the seam allowance, close to the seam.

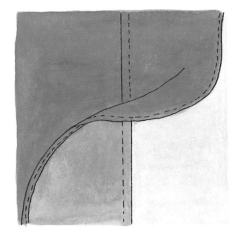

Hand rolling

Working on the wrong side of the fabric, take the edge of the fabric between your thumb and index finger, and roll it over twice. Secure the thread

in the rolled edge, pick up a thread of the main fabric, then slip the needle through the rolled edge. Continue, using small, neat stitches along the length of the fabric.

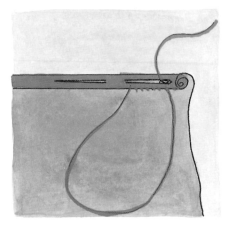

BEADING

Long, fine beading needles are used for sewing small beads onto fabric, as well as strong cotton or polyester thread. Run a little beeswax over the thread before using to strengthen it. Taking a small length of thread, knot the end, and work two or three stitches into the fabric to secure it. Bring the needle to the front of the fabric, thread on the bead, and reinsert the needle close to where it emerged. Secure the bead with a couple of small stitches placed next to it. Repeat this process for all of the beads.

PATCHWORK

Patchwork is the method of joining pieces of fabric together with stitching to form a continuous geometric surface. Many shapes can be used, from squares, and diamonds to triangles, and hexagons, or strips in numerous configurations. Figure out the size, pattern, and colors of your design. Make templates in cardboard and cut

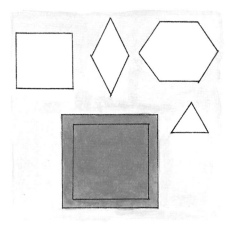

out the shapes from your chosen fabrics with a ¼in (6mm) seam allowance all around. Before you start to sew and pin the patchwork shapes together, arrange them in the correct position so that you can view the impression of the overall design.

Set up the machine for straight stitch and use the presser foot. Align the edge of the fabric with the presser foot and stitch along the shape, securing the start and the end of the stitching with a few stitches backward and forth. Stitch the shapes together to make rows. Press all the seams open. Pin the rows together,

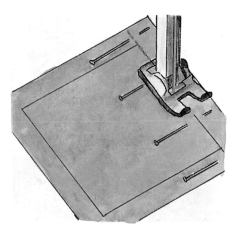

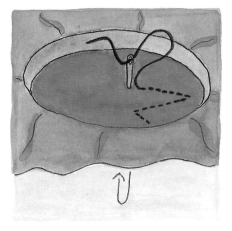

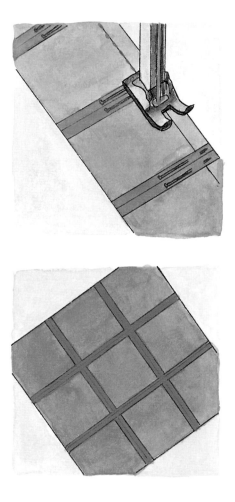

being careful to match all the seams. Stitch the rows together, then press the seams open.

HOW TO QUILT

There are three layers in quilting – the quilt top, the batting and the back. These layers should be basted together securely, working from the middle out to the edges, horizontally, vertically, and diagonally. Stitch four rows of concentric basting to hold the three layers together securely. Mark your quilting pattern on the quilt using tailor's chalk or one of the methods described above. You can use either machine or hand quilting, but for both it is advisable to use a large hoop or frame (at least 14in (35cm) in diameter and ¾in (2cm) deep) as this will help you to maintain an even tension.

Hand quilting
You will need a quilting needle and strong cotton quilting thread, strengthened by running it through some beeswax. Knot the end of a small

length of thread, insert the needle into the quilt, and pull the knot through the backing fabric into the batting. Work a series of small, evenly spaced stab or running stitches. Start in the middle of the design and then work outward, following the quilting pattern. Finish off by tying a knot near the surface of the top layer, then make a small stitch

and pull the knot into the batting, and cut the remaining thread.
Machine quilting with a quilting foot
This is ideal for regular geometric

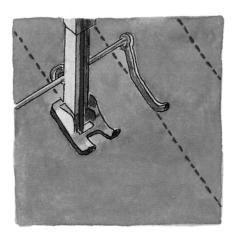

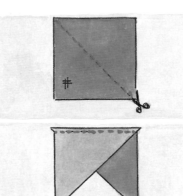

HOW TO MAKE BIAS BINDING

Cut a square of fabric the required size, on the straight grain. Draw a line diagonally across the fabric, dividing it in half, then cut it in half diagonally.

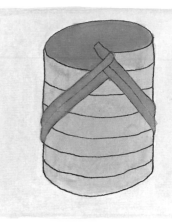

patterns and is quicker than hand quilting. You do not need a frame for this method. Using a quilting thread and running stitch, set the stitch length by stitching a trial piece and varying the stitch width and tension until you have a good result. Start in the middle of the design and work outward, stitching the quilting lines in opposite directions to prevent the layers from slipping.

Machine quilting with a freestyle embroidery foot

This is perfect for more intricate or curved designs. Using the freestyle

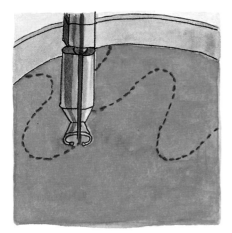

embroidery foot, lower the presser foot to engage the top tension. Lower the feed dog and set the stitch width to zero. Using running stitch, start in the middle of the design. Work outward, following the quilting pattern.

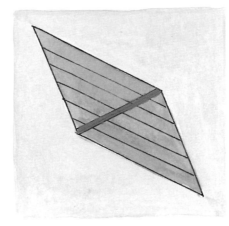

With right sides facing, place the top and bottom edges together, pin and stitch a ¼in (6mm) seam. Trim and press the seam allowance open. With a sharp pencil and a ruler, mark parallel lines across the fabric in the width you require. Pin the diagonal edges together, right sides facing, aligning the top edge of the fabric with the first marked line. Make sure that all the lines match together, then stitch. Trim and press the seam allowance open. Beginning at the top edge, cut along the lines in a continuous spiral until you have managed to make a long strip.

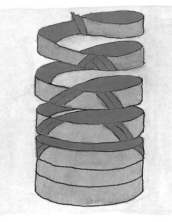

HOW TO BIND EDGES

Press a ¼in (6mm) seam along one edge of the bias strip to the wrong side, and fold in ⅜in (1.5cm) at one end of the strip. With right sides facing and raw edges together, stitch a ½in (12mm) seam beginning in the middle of one side. Stitch to the first corner, ¼in

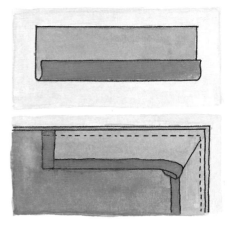

(6mm) from the edge then, leaving the needle in the fabric, raise the presser foot and pivot the fabric around to sew the next edge. A pleat will form in the binding, which you should use to miter the corner. Continue along all of the edges in the same way. When you have reached the end, trim the remaining binding, leaving ⅝in (1.5cm). Fold over a seam and overlap the beginning of the binding. Fold the binding to the back, covering the stitching line, and slipstitch in place. Fold the excess fabric neatly at the corners at a 45° angle, and stitch.

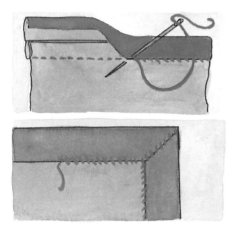

PIPING

Piping consists of bias strips of fabric wrapped around piping cord. Make bias binding the length you need and wide enough to cover the piping cord, with a ⅝in (1.5cm) seam allowance. Lay the

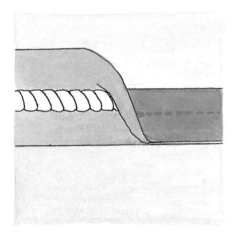

binding wrong side up on a flat surface, place the piping in the middle, and fold over the binding, raw edges together. Pin and stitch close to the cord, using a zipper foot.

INSERTING PIPING

Lay the piping on the right side of one of the fabric pieces, raw edges together.

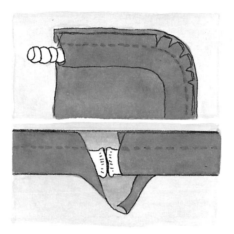

Pin in place. Using a zipper foot, stitch along the seam line, snipping into the seam allowance of the piping around the curves. To join the piping together, stop stitching 2in (5cm) from the beginning of the piping, unpick some of the stitches of the binding strip, and fold it back. Cut the cord so that the ends meet. Then fold the binding back over the cord, overlapping the seams, turn under the edge, and slipstitch in

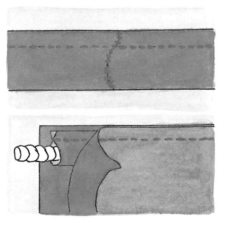

place. Lay the other piece of fabric on top of the piped piece, with right sides together and aligning the edges. Pin and stitch through all the layers along the same seam line.

INSERTING A ZIPPER IN A SEAM

Place the two pieces of fabric together, right sides facing, matching edges and

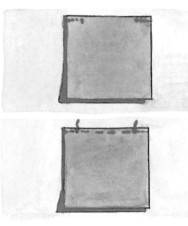

corners. Sew a seam in from each end with the size of the zipper determining the space at each end. Leave an opening for the zipper, baste the opening along the seam line and press the seam open.

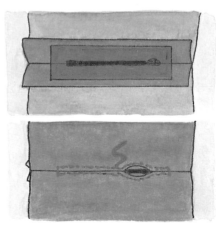

Lay the zipper the wrong side up along the basted edge, and baste in place. Sew it in place from the right side of the fabric using a zipper foot. Take out the basting; open the zipper.

PATTERNS

HOW TO ENLARGE THE PATTERNS

Using a photocopier, scale up the patterns by the following percentages:

Circles Shirt 653%

◆

Flowers Shirt 623%

◆

Man's Vest 431%
small: 40
medium: 42
large: 44

◆

Woman's Vest 382%
small: 8
medium: 10
large: 12

◆

Spirals Hat 410%

◆

Sea Anemones Bag 274%

◆

TEMPLATES

All measurements shown with the templates for each project give the dimensions of the finished piece. Vest templates give the dimensions of the largest size (12 or 44).

HOW TO USE THE PATTERNS

Lay the fabric on a large, flat, clean work surface and have ready tailor's chalk, pins, and needle and thread. Read the information on each pattern piece carefully before you begin to cut your fabric.

The long arrow marked on the pattern pieces indicates the grainline. Place the pattern piece on the straight grain of the fabric, keeping the line parallel to the selvedge or folded edge.

Cut out all the pattern pieces along the cutting line (outer line) indicated for the appropriate size, using sharp dressmaking scissors in long, even strokes.

All markings, darts, and lines of construction should be transferred to the fabric with basting stitches or chalk lines before removing the pattern piece.

Where the pattern instructions read "cut on fold", place the pattern piece edge exactly along the folded edge of the fabric. This edge of the fabric should never be cut. All the patterns include a ⅝in (15mm) seam allowance.

To make sure your garments have a professional finish, press each seam after you have sewn it. The seam should be pressed flat, then pressed open. Trim seams close to the stitching, and trim corners at the tip and on each side. Clip seam allowances, where necessary, so that they lie flat: outer curves should be notched, while inner curves should be clipped.

CIRCLES SHIRT

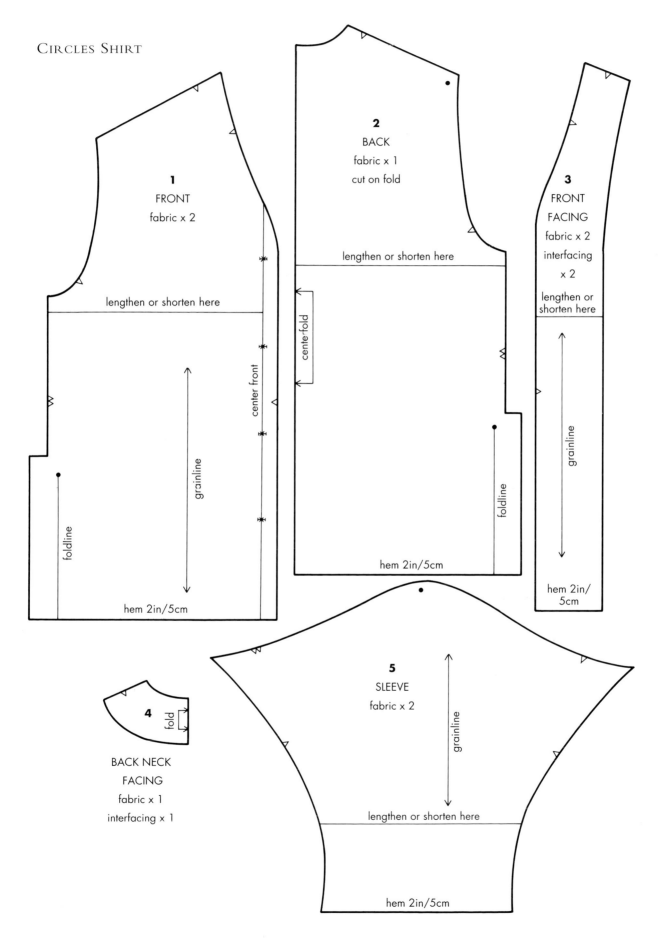

1
FRONT
fabric x 2

lengthen or shorten here

grainline

foldline

center front

hem 2in/5cm

2
BACK
fabric x 1
cut on fold

lengthen or shorten here

center fold

foldline

hem 2in/5cm

3
FRONT
FACING
fabric x 2
interfacing
x 2

lengthen or
shorten here

grainline

hem 2in/
5cm

4
fold

BACK NECK
FACING
fabric x 1
interfacing x 1

5
SLEEVE
fabric x 2

grainline

lengthen or shorten here

hem 2in/5cm

FLOWERS SHIRT

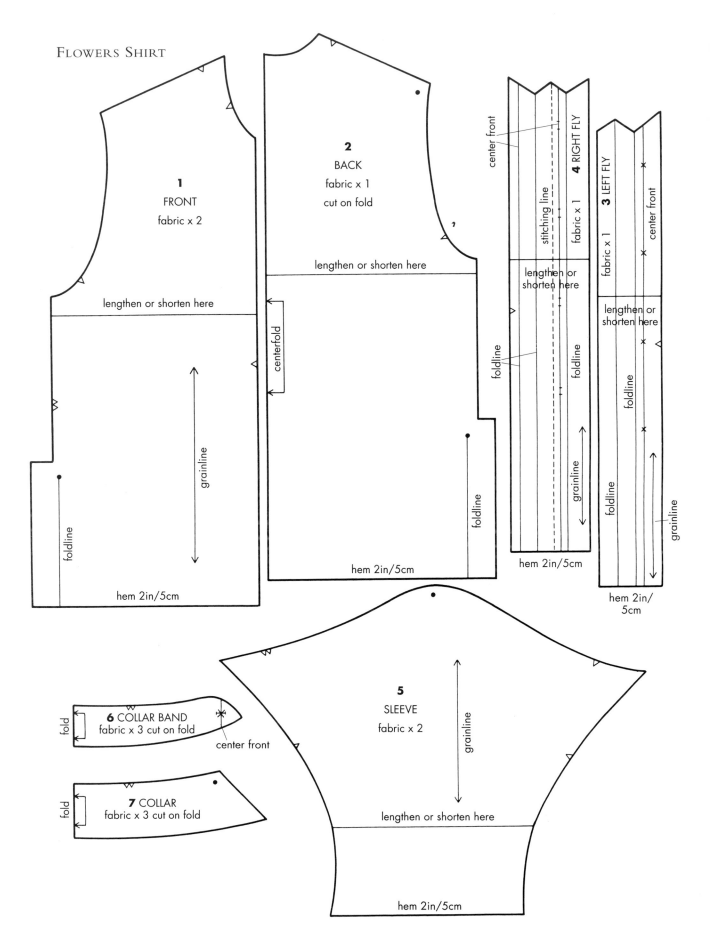

1
FRONT
fabric x 2

lengthen or shorten here

grainline

foldline

hem 2in/5cm

2
BACK
fabric x 1
cut on fold

lengthen or shorten here

centerfold

foldline

hem 2in/5cm

center front

stitching line

4 RIGHT FLY

fabric x 1

lengthen or shorten here

foldline

foldline

grainline

hem 2in/5cm

3 LEFT FLY

fabric x 1

center front

lengthen or shorten here

foldline

foldline

grainline

hem 2in/ 5cm

5
SLEEVE
fabric x 2

grainline

lengthen or shorten here

hem 2in/5cm

fold

6 COLLAR BAND
fabric x 3 cut on fold

center front

fold

7 COLLAR
fabric x 3 cut on fold

MAN'S VEST

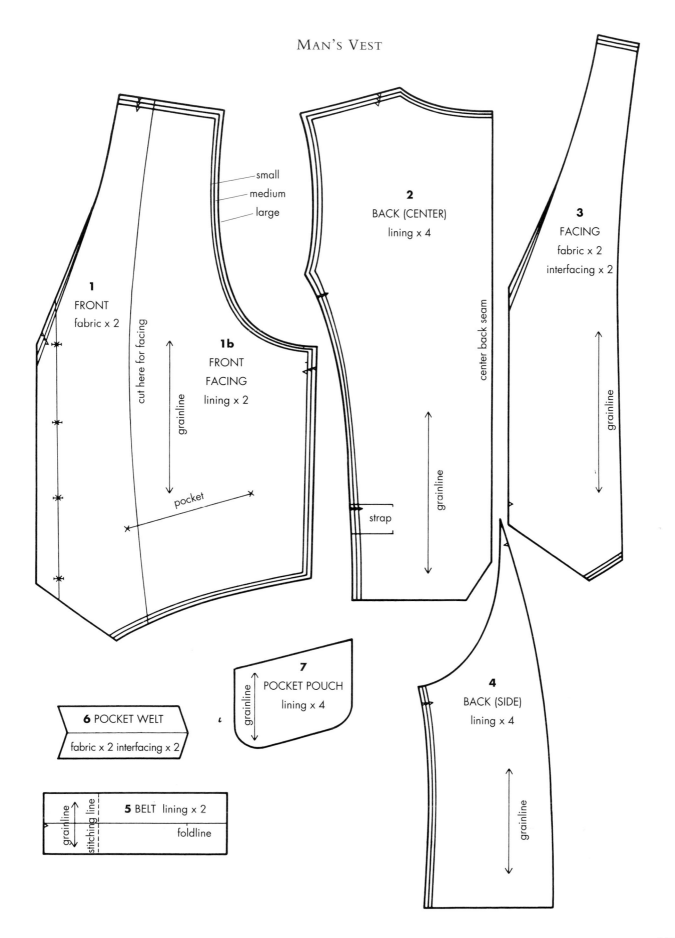

1
FRONT
fabric x 2

cut here for facing

1b
FRONT
FACING
lining x 2

grainline

pocket

small
medium
large

2
BACK (CENTER)
lining x 4

center back seam

grainline

strap

3
FACING
fabric x 2
interfacing x 2

grainline

7
POCKET POUCH
lining x 4

grainline

6 POCKET WELT
fabric x 2 interfacing x 2

5 BELT lining x 2
foldline
grainline
stitching line

4
BACK (SIDE)
lining x 4

grainline

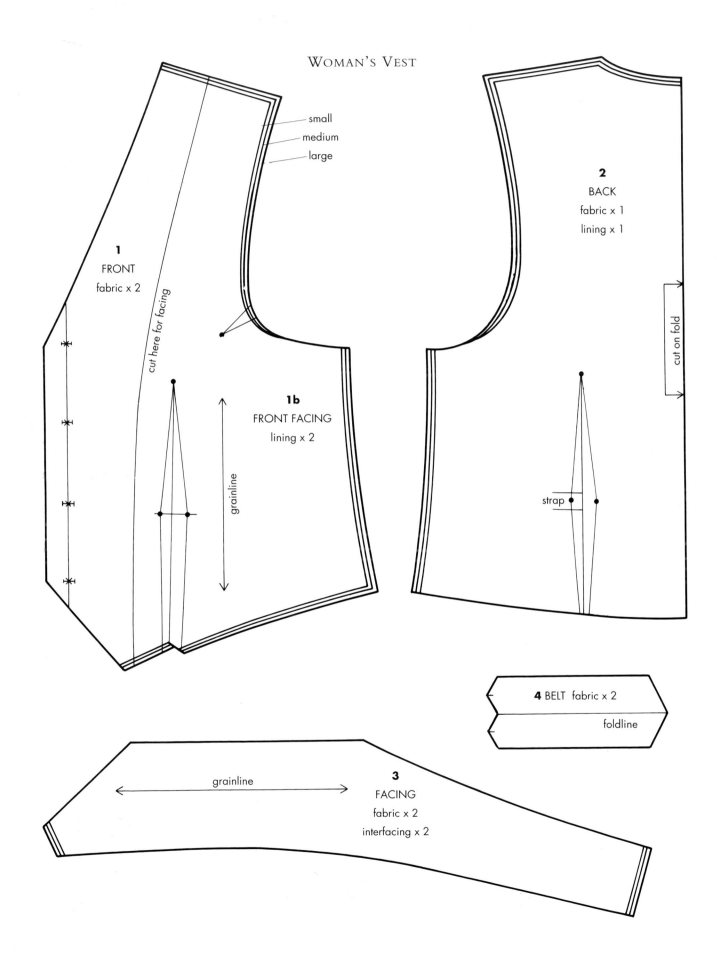

WOMAN'S VEST

small
medium
large

1
FRONT
fabric x 2

cut here for facing

1b
FRONT FACING
lining x 2

grainline

2
BACK
fabric x 1
lining x 1

cut on fold

strap

4 BELT fabric x 2

foldline

grainline

3
FACING
fabric x 2
interfacing x 2

SPIRALS HAT

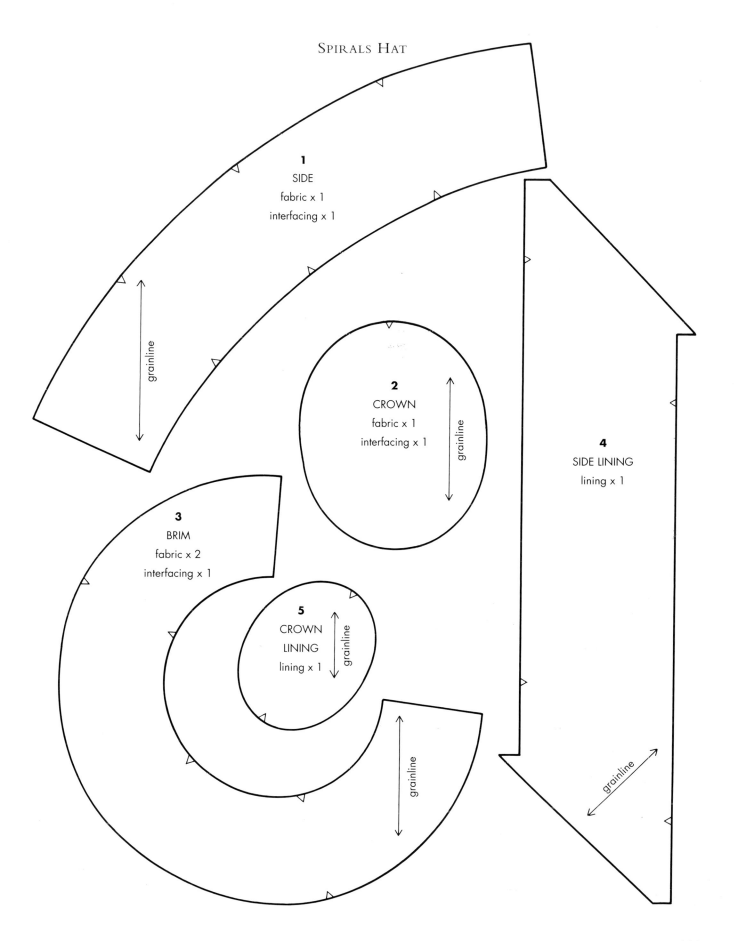

1
SIDE
fabric x 1
interfacing x 1

grainline

2
CROWN
fabric x 1
interfacing x 1

grainline

4
SIDE LINING
lining x 1

3
BRIM
fabric x 2
interfacing x 1

5
CROWN
LINING
lining x 1

grainline

grainline

grainline

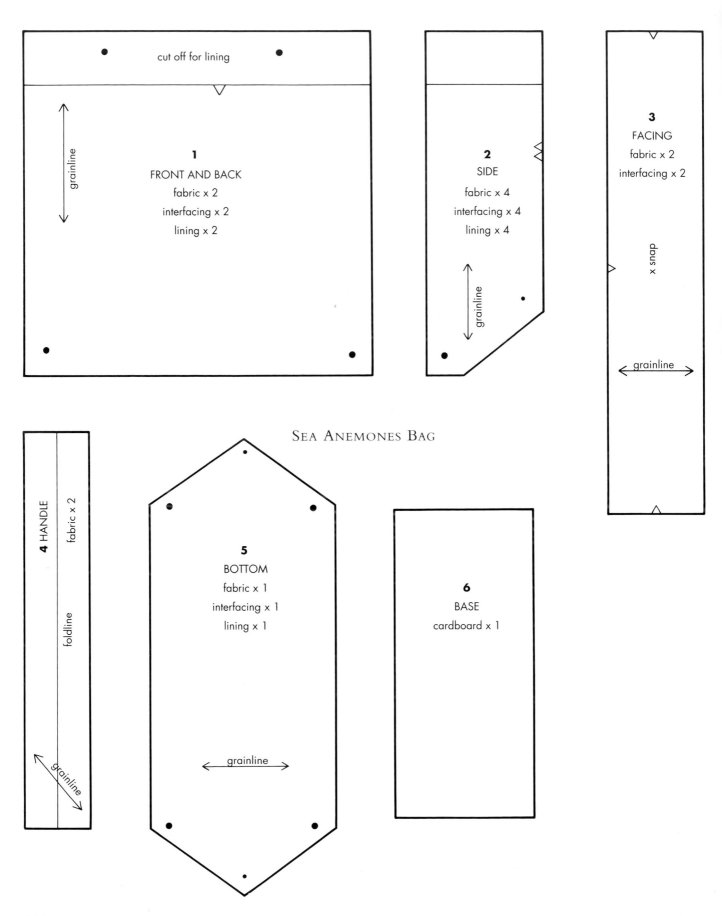

cut off for lining

1

FRONT AND BACK

fabric x 2

interfacing x 2

lining x 2

grainline

2

SIDE

fabric x 4

interfacing x 4

lining x 4

grainline

3

FACING

fabric x 2

interfacing x 2

x snap

grainline

4 HANDLE

fabric x 2

foldline

grainline

SEA ANEMONES BAG

5

BOTTOM

fabric x 1

interfacing x 1

lining x 1

grainline

6

BASE

cardboard x 1

INDEX

SUPPLIERS

Artfabrik
664 West Main Street
Cary
IL 60013
Hand-dyed fabrics and threads

Clotilde, Inc.
2 Sew Smart Way
Stevens Point
WI 54481–80301

Coats & Clark
30 Patewood Drive
Suite 351
Greenville
SC 29615
Metallic, and rayon threads

DMC
107 Trumbull Street
Elizabeth
NJ 07206
Embroidery threads and pearl cotton

Fabric Traditions
1350 Broadway
New York
NY 10018
Multi-purpose fabrics for apparel, quilting, home decorating, and crafts

G Street Fabric
12240 Wilkins Avenue
Rockville
MD 20852
Fabrics (by mail order)

Global Village Importers
1101 SW Washington
Suite 140
Portland
OR 97205–2313
Handwoven cotton fabrics and trim from Guatemala

Gutermann of America Inc.
8227 Arrowridge Boulevard
Charlotte
NC 28273
Hand- and machine-sewing threads, metallic, silk, upholstery, and cotton quilting threads

Hoffman California Fabrics
25792 Obrero Drive
Mission Viejo
CA 92691
Fashion, quilting, and decorator fabrics

Madeira Marketing Ltd
600 East 9th Street
Michigan City
IN 46360
Decorative machine and serger threads

Nancy's Notions
333 Beichl Avenue
Beaver Dam
WI 53916–0683
Specialty presser feet, adhesives, and elastics

National Thread &
   Supply Corp.
695 Red Oak Road
Dept A-202
Stockbridge
GA 30281
Threads, pressing equipment, and notions

Sew Art International
PO Box 550
Bountiful
UT 84010
Unusual threads for machine embroidery

Signature
PO Box 507
Mount Holly
MC 28120

Sulky of America
3113D Broadpoint Drive
Harbor Heights
FL 33983
Rayon and metallic threads

Swiss-Metrosene Inc.
1107 Martin Drive
Roseville
CA 97661
General purpose threads, cotton machine embroidery threads

Tinsel Threads Inc.
Horn of America
PO Box 608
Sutton
WV 26601
Machine embroidery rayon and metallic threads

Treadleart
25834 Narbonne Avenue
Lomita
CA 90717
Sewing and machine embroidery threads; presser feet

VIP Fabrics
1412 Broadway
New York
NY 10018
Multi-purpose fabrics for apparel, quilting, home decorating, and crafts

Web of Thread
3240 Lone Oak Road
Suite 124
Paaducah
KY 42003
Specialty threads, yarn, and cords; color cards

YLI
482 North Freedom
   Boulevard
Provo
UT 84601
Designer and decorative rayon threads

ACKNOWLEDGMENTS

I would like to thank all the people involved in creating this book – particularly Susan Downing and Anthea Snow for their hard work, support, enthusiasm, and humor.

On a personal level, I would like to thank my parents and family, especially my sister Maria, who were always there to give me moral support, love, and reassurance.

Finally, I would like to thank Jonathan Hamilton, who gave me continual support, confidence, and ideas throughout the designing and writing of the book.